More Praise for *Leading Out Loud*

"Leadership isn't a concept that can be described by a simple formula or a set of rules; it's complex, frequently messy, and always deeply personal. Fortunately, Pearce's inimitable style puts it all in perspective. He guides the reader on a journey to first recognize what she stands for and believes in, and then firmly prods her to discover ways to inspire others to action. You'll find *Leading Out Loud* to be a trusted friend, especially during those critical junctures where change is inevitable."

— Michael Nahum, president, Micro Encoder, Inc.

"Anyone who wishes to lead with a capital 'L' would be foolish not read every word Terry Pearce makes available. He understood where leadership was truly going before the word was marginalized. He can help you gain a compass."

—Pip Coburn, founder, Coburn Ventures

"In today's hyper-competitive markets, a leader has to connect with people, or fail to gain the commitment necessary to survive, much less thrive. In three major organizations, *Leading Out Loud* has provided me with a reliable, repeatable blueprint to engage, energize, and fully commit people to the challenging work we face."

—John B. Bunch, CEO, The Mutual Fund Store; former president, Retail Distribution, TDAmeritrade

"I read *Leading Out Loud* while enduring a snowstorm in a small tent in the arctic. I highlighted and tore out key pages as I studied the book. It impacted me in a way that forever changed my communications. I still carry those tattered pages with me. This book taught me how to engage others through connection, not just facts. *Leading Out Loud* is priceless."

—Matt Hyde, president and CEO, West Marine

"A leader's ability to communicate authentically is the single most important tool for initiating change successfully rather than impeding it. In this remarkable book, Terry Pearce shows how you can inspire commitment and accelerate organizational growth."

—Christopher Rice, CEO, BlessingWhite

"Having developed and coached senior corporate leaders for more than 25 years, I can honestly say that the concepts from *Leading Out Loud* are some of the most powerful, relevant, impactful and applicable of anything I've seen for making leaders more effective in driving engagement and results."

—Jeff Rosenthal, Global Technology Practice Lead, Korn/Ferry Leadership & Talent Consulting

"*Leading Out Loud* has been a revelation in both my professional life and my personal life. I use Terry's principles of authenticity every day, and I find myself returning often to this work as I continue to hone my leadership competencies."

—Thomas S. Murphy, former chief information officer, AmerisourceBergen

"Change and the pressing need for authentic leadership to navigate through it have remained fixtures in the time since *Leading Out Loud* first burst on to the bookshelves. Every day, in every interaction I have, be it with my sons at home, my colleagues at work, or with my racing team at the track, I strive to apply Terry's teachings in how I couch my messages. That is how clear it is to me that this book is an essential guide to communications in life and as a leader. This book will challenge you and if you embrace the principles it spells out, you will emerge with a practical leadership toolkit in your back pocket and the confidence to inspire your team to overcome any obstacle, and truly qualify as an authentic leader."

—John Ure, engineering director, Customer Solutions, SPI Lasers UK Ltd.

"Timeless, practical, and relevant, *Leading Out Loud* always hits the mark. Terry keeps it remarkably simple, yet challenges your inner self to understand and share what you really believe in. The book continues to inspire you to lead. Read it and you'll see what I mean!"

—Mike Blackburn, VP Strategy & Planning, Global Government, BT Global Services

"If you've heard or voiced the complaint, 'Why don't they all get with the strategy? We've analyzed, researched, scenario-planned and published . . . !' read *Leading Out Loud.* Terry Pearce makes very clear you need to be communicating to inspire, not just to instruct. Terry challenges managers to step outside their position title, realizing that it's not about 'management by walking about' but rather 'leadership by talking and listening about' with a basic message of authenticity and personal leadership."

—Ken Simper, director, BlessingWhite Asia-Pacific

"Over the past decade I have traveled to forty countries meeting business leaders. Terry's thoughts and teaching on leadership communication resonate across cultures and across borders for leaders in good times and bad. Leading is never easy but sound advice and lessons learned help us all. Terry delivers his message precisely."

—Ross Dove, managing partner, Heritage Global Partners

Leading Out Loud

Leading Out Loud

A Guide for Engaging Others in Creating the Future

Third Edition, newly revised

Terry Pearce

Foreword by Randy Komisar

General Partner, Kleiner Perkins Caufield & Byers, and author of *The Monk and the Riddle*

JOSSEY-BASS
A Wiley Imprint
www.josseybass.com

Author photo by Laura Diana Lopez, dba Manifessence
Cover design: Jeff Puda

Published by Jossey-Bass
A Wiley Imprint
One Montgomery Street, Suite 1200, San Francisco, CA 94104-4594—www.josseybass.com

Library of Congress Cataloging-in-Publication Data
Pearce, Terry
Leading out loud : a guide for engaging others in creating the future / Terry Pearce; foreword by Randy Komisar. – 3rd ed.
p. cm.
Includes bibliographical references and index.
ISBN 978-0-470-90769-6 (cloth); ISBN 978-1-118-41837-6 (ebk.); ISBN 978-1-118-41544-3 (ebk.); ISBN 978-1-118-43352-2 (ebk.)
1. Leadership. 2. Communication in management. 3. Public speaking. I. Title.
HD57.7.P4 2013
658.4'092–dc23
2012038118

Printed in the United States of America

THIRD EDITION

HB Printing 10 9 8 7 6 5 4 3 2 1

Contents

Dedicated with love and appreciation
for the life of
Jodi Pearce Ehrlicher
1976–2007

and

In memoriam for Jim McNeil,
Ron Pearce,
and
Gene Stone

And for the living,
sons Jeff and Joel Pearce,
and comrade Stephen Hamilton

Foreword

One of my earliest memories of Terry Pearce was when I was invited to speak to his class at the Graduate School of Business at the University of California, Berkeley. It was one of the most popular classes in the school, yet it was in a soft subject for a prestigious graduate business program. I found it somewhat surprising that these MBA students were more interested in my own personal metamorphosis from Harvard lawyer, Silicon-Valley dealmaker, and founder of start-ups than they were in the business formulas for success. When I recognized the emphasis on passion, I knew Terry was onto something meaningful. This was not the usual business school communication class of PowerPoint slides and technique. Terry was asking the students to discover a starting point for what they wanted to change in the world by imploring self-examination of what moved them. The class was far more about inspiration than it was about learning how to sound smart to venture capitalists or corporate recruiters. The first edition of *Leading Out Loud* was already popular, and the class was clearly going far beyond the book's original concepts to a broader inquiry. I thought this was absolutely appropriate, because my experience had suggested that for people to be great, to accomplish the impossible, they need inspiration more than financial incentives. Business to me has always been more about the romance of the big idea than the finance of the exit.

For the last few years, I've been engaged as a Virtual CEO and investing partner at Kleiner Perkins Caufield & Byers, a venerable Silicon Valley venture capital firm. I picture myself as a cloud that surrounds the key management group of a start-up, helping them apply leadership principles, lending my own convictions about the necessity of knowing and implementing the fundamentals of the business. More important, I encourage the group to employ the skills of foraging, finding and inspiring people with the broadest implications of what the business is trying to do in the world as a way of building an enterprise that will have staying power—not just in the market, but in the souls of those who engage in it. I look for missionaries, not mercenaries; entrepreneurs who strive for meaning and significance in their careers and in their lives.

I've been in a few meetings with budding entrepreneurs exploring the question of the sequence of the words *values, value,* and *valuation.* Which of these comes first in those who would institute change in the world? *Values* are the fundamental tenets that you want to express in the enterprise, *value* is what difference your idea will make to the greater good, and *valuation* is what an outside constituency judges your contribution is worth in monetary terms. This seems to be the order that gives the most satisfaction, and the one that actually provides the clearest portent for success.

Many of Terry's clients, like most of my own, are in business. Like most areas of life, business has the potential of being an instrument for positive change. It is a vehicle for creative expression—for changing things for the better, a field for bringing forth an idea that expresses an ideal. Just as artists use a palette and a canvas for this process, business leaders inspire others to interpret a spreadsheet and a marketing projection. Politicians might use their passion to commission a public opinion poll, to interpret the results from a ballot box, their colleagues' reaction to a draft of legislation, or feedback from constituents. In each case, the source of creativity that generates potential for change is within the individual leader and that leader's team.

What Terry has done in *Leading Out Loud* is to name the internal principles that are essential to get beyond the popular to the meaningful, prescribe a process for each person to discover what is inside that prompts that conviction, and then suggest a precise process for getting it out. What makes this work unique is the guidance he provides in getting to what really matters in implementing change.

Terry comments on many distinctions in the work—inspiration and motivation, loyalty and satisfaction, progress and change, results and meaning—yet the one that seems central is his distinction between the French verbs for listening, *écouter* and *entendre.* One implies getting the words and providing an answer, the other grasping the meaning and the essence of the other. Listening for words and answering logically is easy and often not satisfying. Attending to the other is receiving meaning, empathizing, and responding in kind. These distinctions are central to the message of *Leading Out Loud.*

The primary value of this work is that it helps us experience what matters in our desire to lead—it is not more money or even prestige. It is the chance to express a value that is dear to us in a practical way, to institute a legacy of change that will live beyond us and that will inspire others. This can only be accomplished with introspection and discipline, not one or the other, but both. Knowing who we are and finding ways to express ourselves in a way that inspires others to create a different future . . . that is true leadership.

In *Leading Out Loud,* we see principles unfold that are about self-knowledge and empathy, discovering our own values, deepening our emotional awareness, and connecting with others in ways that are not just numbers or opinions. Then Terry introduces the discipline necessary to actually get something done, a Guide to keep us from losing our awareness while also focusing us on the practical. He describes this Guide as a "biography with a purpose." This is an appropriate description of a questioning protocol to discover the essence of what matters in the implementation of any change, whether a start-up, a corporate restructuring, or a change in culture. You, the leader, are at the center of it, and your values and the value the change will deliver will determine how others evaluate it with their hearts as well as their heads. The process of discovery offered by this Guide is invaluable to our ability to inspire. I've often maintained that it takes a different kind of person to lead in various phases of change, and Terry combines the dominant characteristics of that theory into one discipline. In the world of fast-moving start-ups, it's frequently too hectic for all this to unfold, but to strive for such balance and integration is indeed striving for the best of life.

Reading Terry's latest edition brings to mind a powerful challenge from another great writer, Ernest Hemingway. In *A*

Moveable Feast, Hemingway writes, "All you have to do is write one true sentence. Write the truest sentence you know." That is the quest of a lifetime, and in *Leading Out Loud,* Terry helps us find that sentence within ourselves and express it with the full conviction of our mind, heart, and soul.

January 2013 RANDY KOMISAR
Silicon Valley

Preface

The first edition of *Leading Out Loud,* published in 1995, focused on public speaking and emphasized the importance of authenticity. The second edition (2003) expanded the understanding of the principles to include all communication aimed at inspiration, every encounter from the casual conversation at a water cooler or in a war theater to e-mail, voice mail, and cross-cultural video. It also included a framework for a *message platform,* a tool to guide leaders to go deep enough to find the stuff of inspiration—to ask the proper questions to find their own source of meaning in the message.

This third edition of *Leading Out Loud* brings the field of leadership communication up-to-date, offering insights and practica to those who strive to inspire others to take action to effect change. If you have not been introduced to the ideas of leadership communication, you will find that this work stands very well on its own. If you have read an earlier edition of *Leading Out Loud,* you will find a new experience here. This version incorporates principles of the first and second editions, and extends these works with four important additions.

- This edition explores important factors that make leadership communication a distinct skill aimed at inspiration. These distinctions are central to understanding what's needed to hone this skill.
- This edition includes the implications of the remarkable new neuroscientific evidence regarding empathy, impulse control, and brain plasticity. This science shows the possibility of developing characteristics, traits, skills, and perspectives that contribute to the mastery of leadership communication cross-culturally and in various media.

- Revisions to this edition reflect my own further education in mythology and depth psychology, fields that facilitate an understanding of the unconscious movers of our civilization. After the second edition went to press, I completed a degree in these fields with the hope of gaining understanding of the common drivers of inspiration.
- This edition refines and expands the array of tools designed to assist leaders in preparing for the entire range of communication and thereby become more effective in inspiring themselves and others. The message platform introduced in the second edition has been supplemented and refined into the Personal Leadership Communication Guide, a more comprehensive tool that calls for more introspective insights as well as compelling evidence.

This work is also rearranged and supplemented with new stories and examples. The cast of characters has changed a bit to reflect my own change in clientele and emphasis, and I chose to provide a bit more continuity by weaving the same sample Guides throughout the book to help create greater understanding of how a Guide is actually constructed, revised, and developed over time.

In presentations, classes, and readings over the years, I have enjoyed speaking with the book's readers and with consultants around the world who are using *Leading Out Loud* as a source work. Readers and consultants alike invariably ask me about the individuals I reference in the stories and case studies—they are interested in what happened to these people and how they have continued to use the methods and suggestions in the work. I thought it was wonderful that readers considered the material personally, so I'm bringing you up-to-date on the lives of these exemplars as best I can—how what they learned and applied has worked over the years. They are a truly remarkable group.

My challenge, as it is with any author, has been to make this book relevant. The ultimate question is, How does reading this book make a difference? Accordingly, I've tried to keep this work straightforward, accessible, and real. If, as I hope, you find yourself applying what you read here, then I will have met my goals with this new edition.

What's Here?

The nine chapters of the book are presented in two distinct parts. The first four chapters pertain to the internal development of the leader, and the second five chapters are focused on the nature and content of the message.

Making distinctions between the known and the unknown is a wonderful way to learn. The introduction to Part One takes up the task of clarifying the distinctions that make the target clear to the reader. The differences between motivation and inspiration are central to this approach. Clearly one is extrinsic—carrot and stick—and the other is intrinsic, coming from within and involving meaning. Underlying this fundamental pair are words representing concepts that can either compete or complement. For example, *change* can be fear-inducing, upsetting, and psychologically demotivating. (Remember when you *changed* schools when moving to that new town, state, or country?) Yet *progress* is heard as forward-looking, beneficial, and potentially exciting. With each pair, both are necessary, one to operate the organization and achieve your objectives, the other to inspire the greatest engagement and ownership in those involved in creating needed shifts in operation.

Chapters One through Four develop the principles the leader needs in order to communicate with these distinctions in mind. Discovering What Matters is the prerequisite to communicating from a sense of purpose and is the subject of Chapter One. The second principle has been broadened to Deepening Emotional Awareness and Chapter Two explores new material that neurobiologists have developed in the past few years, going well beyond the psychology of emotion to include the hard physiological brain research and its social implications. The chapter explicates the nature of empathy, how that capability can be developed, and also looks at the biology of reaction versus response. Enhancing this area of relating is central to leadership that inspires. As it turns out, human beings can always discern one another's intentions, albeit not always consciously. Ignoring this discernment results in a spaghetti-wired web of pretense characterized by lack of clarity, lack of trust, and (in practical business terms), lack of ability to compete.

Connecting With Others, the third principle, is described in Chapter Three, which explores the power of the narrative forms of mythology, story, and personal experience and the universal import of symbol and image, metaphor and analogy. Chapter Four emphasizes the need for Disciplining the Voice. Because of the proliferation of new vehicles for communication and the myriad opportunities to communicate (some conscious and with forethought and some involuntary or nearly so), it is ever more incumbent on leaders to formulate ideas, feelings, stories, and experiences. Unfortunately, the concept of a message platform has been used in the corporate and political worlds to help leaders "stay on message." Professionals create the central themes and sound bites, and devise ways to return to these themes without regard to the forum or the question asked—so often that listeners often wonder, "Didn't you just say that?"

As noted, the message platform of the second edition has evolved to the Personal Leadership Communication Guide. Far from a series of sound bites, the Guide is a complete, well-considered organic document, created and constantly updated by the leader who uses it, and it incorporates all the passion, facts, experiences, stories, metaphors, and evidence to weave the mosaic of urgency and progress inherent in any attempt to forge a future different from the present. Because it flows through and from the leader, it is highly personal and authentic. It can be used in all circumstances, for all audiences, and in any forum using any media. The Guide reflects a more complete communication, focused not only on the messages themselves but also on the leader's motivations and emotions.

The components and content of this Guide are the subjects of the second part of the book, Chapters Five through Nine. Chapter Five focuses on competence and trust, the prerequisites for any communication to be heard and deeply felt. Here I explore what kind of communication actually conveys empathy, what facts and impressions are necessary to convey competence, the value of gratitude, the revelation of personal motivation, and the search for and revelation of vulnerabilities. Chapter Six takes up the building of shared context, including not just the history of an issue, but the broader implications of the necessity for change. How does one decide on priority? What are the stakes? And most important, where did you (the leader developing the Guide) come in—at what point did you discover this issue and how does the status quo affect you? All these questions are contextual, vital to understand, and vital to understanding. Chapter Seven looks at how a leader imagines and then conveys a state not yet in existence. Is prophecy an act of prediction or creation? Chapter Eight is about action, first how the organization must proceed and then a revelation of what you are willing to do to make your own conviction about the future a reality. Only when you have decided what you are willing to risk and declared it do you have the right, indeed the obligation, to ask others to follow. Chapter Nine discusses how authenticity, competence, and connection can be sustained in various communication channels, including initial presentations or speeches, question-and-answer sessions, informal discussions, and in particular in the electronic networks of e-mail, voice mail, video, and web-based conferences. Finally, the Epilogue emphasizes the current desperate need to break with convention and practice authentic communication in international discourse as well as everyday personal interaction. If there is, as there seems to be, a paucity of understanding and community, this practice could help us all move into a more sustainable world.

Two appendixes supplement the material in the text. The first provides information on the choice and use of evidence in leadership communication. The second presents the framework for preparing your own Personal Leadership Communication Guide. The appendixes are followed by the notes and a recommended reading list.

Leading Out Loud is laced with stories that are highly personal. I feel so strongly that leadership is absolutely personal that I simply couldn't write this work from any other point of view. I still can't go to Washington, D.C., without wending my way around the Tidal Basin to the Jefferson Memorial to reread his immortal words—"We hold these truths to be self-evident"—and then move on to the other quotations of this amazing futurist dreamer. It was personal to Jefferson, just as many centuries earlier it was personal to Lao Tzu, Siddhartha, Mohammad, Jesus, and the founders of all religions. It was personal to Martin Luther King, Steve Jobs, Anwar Sadat, Margaret Thatcher, Nelson Mandela, John Kennedy, and Thomas

Watson. It was also personal to Osama Bin Laden. In all cases, these leaders' declarations came from their beliefs, their times, and their hopes for the future. They were deeply felt and very personal, and they have been taken up by millions since their utterance.

Yes, leadership is personal, and that is no more evident than in descriptions of a future that exists only in the leader's own mind. This is no prediction for the leader; it is the first act of creation.

Who Should Read This Book?

This edition has been written during very trying and yet exciting times in the world. We are in the throes of a financial crisis; new freedoms are being born in countries in the Middle East and Africa; China is emerging as a dominant geopolitical force. India, Brazil, and a new Russia are moving into world prominence with their economic growth. Nearly everyone on the globe is at some level reassessing what is important, what is essential, and what is absolutely unnecessary. We are in a virtual cauldron of change, and leaders are emerging to influence the outcome in their own favor or in favor of their own values. Information is accumulating so fast and is so universally accessible that it can be used by anyone to serve or to manipulate.

But the most important information is not online, it is felt somewhere right under your sternum. Accordingly, you don't have to sit in a corner business office or be a public politician to benefit from this book. Nearly everything written is in some way an advocacy for change, an arrow meant to pierce a metaphorical heart with such force as to cause shifts in possibility. If you feel deeply about the need for progress in any field, or if you want to discover more about how people emerge to lead change, *Leading Out Loud* will prove valuable to you. It is meant to support the revelation of the human soul, vulnerability, and courageous action to bring people together rather than surrendering to petty partisanship and self-aggrandizement. If you want to stir yourself or any others to make a difference in this world, I believe what's here will benefit you. I hope it helps you step up, and gives you confidence to keep doing so.

January 2013 TERRY PEARCE
Larkspur, California

Prologue

Leading Out Loud is a continuing story of the discovery and documentation of the distinct field of leadership communication. My thinking on this began in the early 1990s on a rock in Northern California, where three or four evenings a week I would sit under a darkening sky and write about my experience of consulting with executives and politicians. On Fridays, I would teach a leadership communication elective at the Haas Graduate School of Business, University of California, Berkeley. More often than not, the content for any given class would come right out of my experience of the preceding week. It was not a very scholarly process by academic standards, but it seemed important to the students; they were completely engaged and continued to make the course a popular, hard-to-get ticket.

What I had stumbled and bumbled onto was a coin of the realm for inspiration, and I had applied it with some discipline to the field of leadership. It turned out to be difficult to articulate, and even more difficult to teach. After I spoke at Stanford University's Executive Breakfast in 1992, one of the faculty asked me to identify the sources of my body of work. I was not even sophisticated enough in those days to understand that his question went to the heart of academic credibility. The only names I could think of wrote in fields seemingly far from the practical day-to-day world of business or politics. Rather, they wrote on philosophy, religion, and literature, most of it with a strong mystical bent reaching inside the metaphysical, and that perspective oriented much of my work. Fortunately, I had a history in operational business and politics, having had my hands on the levers of a few organizations, so I was confident in the practicality of the work. That was twenty years ago, and my credentials have improved in the interim. But without that original naïveté, I probably would not have had the courage to write at all.

Leading Out Loud deals with leadership communication as a unique practice, separate from our ability to merely get things done. It deals in our ability to *lead*—measured not only by our competence and what we accomplish but primarily by our ability to communicate who we are and what we stand for in this life.

In 1995, according to *Books in Print,* the words *authentic* and *leader* appeared together only in one work, *Authentic Leadership* by Robert Terry. Dr. Terry's work was an inspiration to me, so the word *authentic* was in the subtitle of the first edition of *Leading Out Loud;* I believe it was only the second work to use the two terms together. Today, seventeen years later, a Google search on the phrase "authentic leadership" yields 1,810,000 hits. In fact, at a recent conference in San Francisco, someone asked, "What word do you wish would disappear from the leadership lexicon?" One of my table mates immediately said, "authentic." The comment might indicate that the once-novel term "authentic leadership" has become a cliché. Yet clichés are born of truth. Authenticity—knowing your values and being able to communicate through their prism—is central to leadership communication.

Shortly after the book's publication in 1995, the principles of *Leading Out Loud* were incorporated into an intensive executive course on authentic communication currently represented and sold by BlessingWhite, one of the leading leadership consulting companies in the world. Participants in the course come to understand the personal nature of leadership and focus on the development of a broad-gauged and deep Communication Guide. This requires introspection, courage, and persistence. It requires finding and building the courage to not only give voice to the change message but also to develop the skill of connecting with others in a way that will inspire them to engage with the ideas and passion of the leader.

Since its inception, this program has reached thousands of leaders and potential leaders of all stripes in all parts of the world. Through the coursework, my classes at the Haas School of Business and the London Business School, my work with individuals, and the worldwide incorporation of these principles by BlessingWhite, we have seen leaders emerge, each from a personal crucible of life, to find new ways of expressing themselves and new ways of engaging others in efforts to make the world a better place.

The field of leadership communication has continued to expand, and others have contributed immensely to its legitimacy. Many excellent scholars and practitioners have now included a perspective on communication in the body of other works on leadership. Nonetheless, actual understanding of the full nature of communication from one human to others—the elements, objective and sublime, of such communication—have been and remain obscure. When we add the kicker of inspiration and its universality, our understanding is even more meager—in fact, it remains a mystery. The third edition of *Leading Out Loud* explores this mystery and adds insight and practical ideas to help leaders bridge that gap of understanding more completely.

When I was writing the second edition, I was also encountering situations in teaching and consulting that required more than a superficial understanding of what it meant to lead across cultures. At the time, popular training emphasized learning languages and differences in etiquette. I knew there was more to it than the blind application of social rules, but I found myself relying more on formulas than real insight, which felt neither accurate nor authentic. So after the book's publication, I slowed my consulting business to a crawl and enrolled in a graduate program in comparative mythology, with an emphasis in depth psychology, at the Pacifica Graduate Institute in Santa Barbara, California. The campus archives house the library and papers of Joseph Campbell, as well as those of the late archetypal psychologists James Hillman, Marianne Woodman, and others. The school enjoys frequent visits by and engagement with Jungian scholars from around the world. I hope this edition reflects a more global perspective as a result of my education both at the Institute and in the world since. I was not exactly a neophyte in therapeutic access to the unconscious—in fact, I was experienced. But my exposure to this curriculum was the stuff of revelation to me. What goes on below the surface of our consciousness affects us far more than anything that reaches our awareness.

The graduate school experience excited substantial curiosity about the nature of inspiration itself. Accordingly, in 2006, I put together the Forum on Cross-Cultural Inspiration. More than seventy people came to San Francisco from several countries—professionals from social organizations, governments, business, the arts, and academia—to explore the subject for four days in group conversation looking through four distinct lenses—neurobiology, mythology, depth psychology, and spirituality. Throughout the forum, the focus was on action in the world—in business, politics, religion, and social service. The extensive white paper from those four days of work also informs this book.

Finally, I've had twists and turns of my own that have made the depth of the material even more important to me. I lost my thirty-one-year-old daughter Jodi to a brain aneurism in late 2007. She was one of the healthiest people I knew, and left a husband and two small children. Her cards and notes still grace the front of my refrigerator. As many of you know, death makes the urgency of life real, and I now have even less patience for manipulation and less-than-passionate leadership, or less-than-passionate living for that matter. Jodi is probably applauding that last sentence from somewhere, even as I write it.

I realize that the arc of history is very long and very deep, and from the early shaman to the modern scientist, our longings and impulses have been consistent, only the stories have changed. I know too that personal experience is singular—while it might point a finger in a certain direction, it does not provide a map for the universal. Accordingly, I've tried to shore up my assertions in a way that will facilitate your own experience. I know that the complexity of theory and practice can sound daunting (I know it does to me) yet some complexity and mystery is central to our understanding about what moves us. I hope this observation serves as an effective guide for your own understanding.

Part One

Leadership Communication: Personal Awareness and Competing Dynamics

In 2004 a friend invited me to participate in a forum at the University of California, Irvine. The two-day agenda featured an address by and some interaction with His Holiness, the fourteenth Dalai Lama. About fifty of us, most from the business world, had lunch together while His Holiness was addressing a corps of the faculty in another building. Our host asked us to formulate some questions for the monk and submit them on note cards—he was to choose a few, and the originator was to ask the question personally.

The auditorium was cleared for security and the Dalai Lama entered with his usual grin and flourish, wearing a visor with the UC Irvine mascot displayed. He spoke to us for a few minutes, but was eager to get to the questions.

I was shocked to hear my name called first. I had listened to His Holiness several times, read many of his works, and simply wanted some solid advice about how to live, given his teachings about compassion and peace. His response: "Do whatever you can to create institutional behavior that will promote cooperation and coexistence." Then he looked right at me and declared, "There is always a leader. One person begins everything. That has to be you."

This idea is not new, but neither is it in vogue. Many extol the idea of "leading from the middle," or "leading by consensus," and while there is popular appeal in both, neither of these ideas have resonance with history. I believe His Holiness was emphasizing the need for a starter, for one person to be of courage, to state the need for change and begin the process. He himself, of course, mounted a pony at the age of twenty-four and led his people into exile. We can see in the recent revolutions in the Middle East—the "Arab Spring"—that leadership did not immediately rise to the fore. There *was* an instigator, as His Holiness predicted. Wael Ghonim, a former Google executive then on sabbatical, actually started the revolution, suggesting on his originally anonymous Facebook page that young people assert themselves on a national day of protest. Later arrested and released, Ghonim remained in Egypt as a spokesperson for some in the revolution (primarily young people) but the revolution itself has been co-opted by other interest groups seeking to install themselves in the place of the previous despot. It took more than a year to elect a president in Egypt, and as of late 2012, he still does not have full popularly-supported presidential authority—no one has yet crystalized and spoken for those wanting freedom in a way that expresses a set of principles. I can't help but contrast this circumstance to those in play when Anwar Sadat led by traveling to the Knesset to solidify a peace with Israel. He led with all his heart, against the advice of his closest friends and family, and took the definitive action that cost him his life. This urge, this conviction, was inside him, not just as an idea but as something that identified him as a man.

As I write, we in the United States are currently experiencing the "Occupy" movement, again with no leaders to state and extol a set of principles in a way that would actually represent change. What we see is a narrow coalition of dissatisfied people expressing their anger and frustration in the public square. Will anything come of it? I think that the Dalai Lama suggests that the answer is "Not until someone steps up to take the lead in a new order of things"—not just rabble-rousing or complaining about the status quo but declaring something new, something growing from a set of principles that reside in the heart of the leader. These principles need to be awakened in others.

Doing so in today's world requires communication that is substantially different from what was needed only a decade ago. Recent research by the leadership consulting company Blessing-White indicates that when asked what characteristics are most desirable in leaders, followers favor empathy, business competence, trustworthiness, external attunement, and depth.[1] Leaders still communicate the facts, the information that is necessary to make and implement a decision. For this, leaders have to be logical, suggesting that moving from where we are to where we are going is a needed, cogent, and doable change. More important, they also must constantly communicate the why—what makes the action meaningful—and by doing so, engage others more deeply. Whether they are heading up a volunteer effort, a business, a club, a theater, an orchestra, a city, a country, or a revolution, leaders must include the emotional and the spiritual implications of the actions they advocate, and those implications must live in the soul of the leader. These are internal necessities, the personal awareness that must be in place. Such integrated communication not only conveys consistency with the goals and strategy of the organization or movement, it also suggests consistency with the values of the leader and the organization.

The distinctions that separate leadership communication from operational communication reflect the difference between a set of instructions and an internal connection. My purpose in discussing these is to discover the substantive differences in communication that inspire rather than merely motivate. Extensive research suggests that we perform much more effectively when we are inspired than when we are merely motivated by rewards or punishments.[2] Indeed, most of us understand the difference intuitively. The essence of inspiration is, as Joseph Campbell offered, not only in the meaning of life but in the "experience of living." It is up to the leader to bridge the gap between doing and being, between dreams and the actions that make those dreams real. Commitment and passion enable us to cross that emotional bridge.

Like it or not, *commitment* and *passion* are spiritual words. They are not generated from the body or the mind. We do not merely figure out commitment; it is an integrated phenomenon, encompassing our entire selves, mind and heart. Commitment gives rise to passion, the driving and exciting force in which meaning reveals itself. A real surge of excitement comes with knowing that you can actually make a difference in the world. We need only to look to our volunteer activities to discover that we are committed to what we believe in, to the causes that create meaning in our lives. Is this too much to ask of our country or our company? Not at all. In fact, great organizations with good leadership provide lots of opportunity for such expression, right in the public square or in the workplace.

Where do passion and commitment reside? In *inspiration.*

How do we access this inspiration in ourselves? Like other somewhat ethereal and less accessible goals, this elevated state is elusive when approached directly, but when we are able to point in the right direction, we often see what it is *not,* and we are therefore led to it indirectly. One method of access is to assess competing dynamics, one of which is more logical, digital, and direct, while the other dynamic, the one we are seeking, tends to be more flowing, analog, and emotional. Two pairs are central to a leader's success: first, change and progress, and next, compliance and commitment.

The leader is not a "change agent," as often declared in the popular literature, but is rather a "creator of progress." The distinction between these two is the communication lifeblood of the effective leader. There is adequate psychological data to prove that on the whole people hate change; it can seem whimsical, upsetting, and without purpose. Change does not necessarily have a positive direction—it can put us out of our routine and leave us without bearings. Change can also be associated with a lack of ability to control our own environment. Change as such seems imposed, by some authority or by chance, rather than being self-generated, and it is often felt as having unpleasant consequences. The word *change* connotes short-term and perhaps temporary conditions that may seem negative.

As much as people hate change, almost everyone loves *progress*—it connotes moving forward toward a condition or set of circumstances that is new and favorable. Progress is an agreed-to positive result of change. The difference between change and progress can be communicated by the leader who has thought through the implications of change against a set of values and a desirable future. Only then is it reasonable to expect to make progress toward resolving the second set of competing dynamics, compliance and commitment, favorably.

Compliance, of course, implies an outside power commanding obedience. This may sound harsh, but whether it is the voice of your boss, your parent, the police department, or the tax collectors, the dynamic is one of you doing what is required. It is quite possible for an individual to convert this other-motivated action to an internally inspired one, transforming the experience of obeying to one of contributing from the heart. Are we internally dedicated to the values of our company? Do we respect our parents' judgment over our own? Are we internally convinced of the value of the rule of law and therefore willing to give up some freedoms for the principle? Do we really believe in contributing some of our wealth to the public good through a democratically elected set of officials in order to support the community, even as we understand that some of our tax money may well be squandered? If the answers to these questions are "Yes," then we are voluntarily committed to principles rather than compliant to authority.

It is the leader's job to communicate in such a way that the supporting values are clear, that people have an opportunity to be fully invested in the outcome of their actions. Such communication necessarily has to do with the principles at stake, the goals they are trying to jointly achieve, and how the leader's own personal values are aligned with the greater purpose. Such reflection will allow the leader to inspire commitment rather than merely motivate compliance. Doing so takes a great deal of introspection.

In March 2010, William Deresiewicz, American writer, literary critic, and former Yale professor, addressed the plebe class at the U.S. Military Academy at West Point. In his remarks (titled "Solitude and Leadership" and later printed in *American Scholar*) he made some observations about what leadership is *not:* "Leadership and aptitude, leadership and achievement, leadership and even excellence have to be different things; otherwise the concept of leadership has no meaning."[3] He further decried the way leaders have been seen in society as "people who can climb the greasy pole of whatever hierarchy they decide to attach themselves to."

As Deresiewicz implies, this was not an effective characterization. Rather, he asserts that leadership is about the courage and discipline to think things through for ourselves and the moral courage to stand up for what we believe to be right. He then asserts, and I agree with him, that self-knowledge can only be gained through introspection, frequently in solitude. In short, he argues for reading books rather than e-mail, for reflection as much as conversation, and for as much solitude and focus as it takes to discover who we are and what we will stand for. Only then can we decide how to deploy our own character in the world. Only then will we have the ability to distinguish for ourselves, and then for others, the differences that will make commitment rise.

The distinctions between change and progress and compliance and commitment are proxies for the distinction between motivation and inspiration. There are others: for example, we can articulate and communicate the strategy of our enterprise, but can we articulate the values that call that strategy forward? We can have tremendous clarity about where we are going, but can we transmit the depth of what we are up to? We can define what results we want to accomplish, but can we convey the meaning in accomplishing those goals—meaning that actually makes a difference in the quality of how we live and how our efforts create the same meaning for others? We may be able to articulate the institutional objective of our action, but can we also convey our personal motivation in accomplishing that objective? We can point logically to the right thing to do, but can we also align that action with the emotional and perhaps spiritual payoff in doing it? And finally, do we generate mere satisfaction from those who engage, or do they have a sense of loyalty to the leader and the cause?

These are the fundamental differences that define leadership communication: change and progress, strategy and values, clarity and depth, results and meaning, institutional objectives and personal motivation, logical payoffs and emotional and spiritual rewards, and satisfaction and loyalty. By communicating in a way that integrates these dynamics, a leader demonstrates both competence and trustworthiness, and can then inspire rather than motivate, creating commitment rather than mere compliance.

The four chapters that follow take up the four principles to be employed to develop the capacity for such authentic leadership communication. The first three—"Discovering What Matters," "Deepening Emotional Awareness," and "Connecting with Others"—form the basis for the leader's internal development, while the fourth, "Writing–Applying Discipline to Authenticity," describes the documentation process of the Personal Leadership Communication Guide.

Chapter One

Discovering What Matters

The raw material of leadership communication is something besides flesh, bone, and expertise in a field. To inspire others means not only developing the talent to operate in a given domain, but also cultivating the character traits, habits, and internal response patterns that attract others' engagement. Those who get it right stand out.

I first met Gary Fiedel at a spiritual retreat in the early 1980s. In quiet conversation, I learned that he was an accountant in a town very near my own home, and I learned about his background in the streets of Brooklyn. Gary's were not the suburban streets but the streets that had walk-up apartments not far from Coney Island. When Gary was in his teens, he met some friends who had fairly rough ideas of what life was about. Within a few years, his life was on a track that might well have ended in some kind of violence, perhaps in the Brooklyn pool hall where he was a partner or some other place of street worship.

During some particularly dangerous times, Gary had the good sense to take a trip to Los Angeles to visit with one of his old associates who had escaped the neighborhood. His friend had become an accountant, and—through what Gary says was "sheer good luck"—he was able to apprentice with his friend, and over the next few years move to Northern California and set up his own small accounting practice. He married and had a son. The marriage ended in divorce, Gary went on a pre-midlife spiritual quest, and we ended up at the same retreat in the basement of a San Francisco church.

I shared a little of my own frustration with Gary. I too was divorced, and I too was in the very early stages of setting up a small business. But unlike Gary, I worried every day whether the ATM would give me the minimum $20. Aside from a little prayer that I said in front of that banking altar every couple of days, I felt I had no control over my cash flow or revenue stream. A week after the retreat, Gary arrived unannounced at my office door, pulled a few files from the single-drawer cabinet, and told me he would bring them back in a week. When he did, he delivered my first set of financial reports, and gave me instructions to send him my cash receipts, my checkbook register, and my credit card bills every month. He said he would bill me when I could afford it.

This was an extraordinary act of faith, and I never forgot it. When I called Gary's house to thank him, I connected with an old-style answering machine with a new-style message: "Hi, this is Gary, and this is not an answering machine, it is a questioning machine! The two questions are, 'Who are you?' and 'What do you want?'" Then there was a pause, and the message added, "and if you think those are trivial questions, consider that 95 percent of the population goes through life and never answers either one!"

I have later heard that greeting attributed to various people, but it was Gary Fiedel's version that stuck with me. Gary is still at his post, some thirty years later, and those questions still ring true. While I certainly had enough life experience to suggest that I was searching for the answers to those questions, I had never asked them explicitly. I was surprised and inspired by the power of the questions in my own life, and now I find them indispensable to my work with would-be or actual leaders. Leaders simply must know their own values if they are to inspire others. Gary's "questioning machine" was a reminder. I had had an inkling a few years earlier.

Who Are You?

I started my first career with IBM in San Francisco and was fortunate to have an upstanding, experienced older manager, David Gaisford. Dave frequently focused us on meaningful questions that to a twenty-six-year-old upstart sounded unnecessarily deep. Our crew of salespeople would meet once a week in a large conference room to share stories of the preceding week. At one such meeting, Dave posed the question, "Who are you?" He asked us to write down our discoveries and then share them around the table. I remember starting to perspire as my peers began to write. I was the youngest at the table, and did not want to have to speak first. Fortunately, the gauntlet started six or seven people in front of me, so by the time it was my turn, I had heard the drift of the conversation—what seemed to be a safe and appropriate response—and was prepared to ape my somewhat older colleagues. As fate would have it, the person to my right was an older member of the group, a man of about forty named Ed McDannell. Ed had been in Vietnam in the Navy and had seen significant combat action in the Mekong Delta.

The generally accepted responses kept coming. One by one, the salespeople shared who they were. Nearly all of the answers reflected roles that they played in life or hobbies that they enjoyed: "I'm a husband," "I'm a father," "I'm a baseball fan," "I'm a loving son." I felt very safe—until it was Ed's turn.

He looked up at the group, scanned the room, and with penetrating eyes and a clear voice, and from a place of his experience of war, he simply and firmly said, "I am a free man!" and put down his paper.

The room was quiet, and I immediately felt my skin start to moisten. I was trapped with no identity that meant anything at all. Ed had raised the bar higher than I could jump, but my embarrassment was not about what I had listed on my paper, it was about my failure to understand the question at its root. I've never made that mistake again. Values trump the roles you might play in your life . . . not the other way around.

What Do You Want?

Many years after IBM and only a couple of years after my encounter with Gary, I met William Miller, at the time manager of the Program on Innovation at Stanford Research Institute. William has since published several books on innovation and creativity; he now consults on global values-based innovation from his home in India.

As we drank coffee around a bistro table, William suggested that "What do you want?" really means, "What are you here to do?" and I quickly saw his point. Having spent my adult life in the San Francisco Bay Area, I was treated, long ago, to the *San Francisco Chronicle* columns of Eric Hoffer, philosopher-cum-longshoreman, whose longest-lived aphorism is "You can never get enough of what you don't need to make you happy." William's corollary to Gary's questions reflects this added insight. People who will successfully lead progress are concerned not only with their personal needs but also with making a difference in the lives of others, and in the life of an organization or a group moving toward a specific new future. The character of the individual, not any physical or emotional wants, is central to this ability to lead.

William went on to tell me of a test that he uses with prospective clients. During the initial interview, he casually reaches into his briefcase and places three books on the desk. Two are about some facet of the field of the prospect (say, business or public administration); the third is a work about the human condition (such as psychology, philosophy, or spirituality). "Invariably," says William, "whenever I'm facing someone I end up working with, the prospect will ignore the works about the field of endeavor and ask about the other, and it doesn't seem to matter in which order the books are stacked!" This is a good sign that the potential leader is interested in values, not merely techniques that have been effective in a given field. Such a leader is interested in making progress happen from a firm human foundation.

But to even define progress, we have to have a sense of qualitative difference or value—of what we will stand for. The ability to find, articulate, and translate our identity depends largely on our maturity in life and on our experience, as it requires reflection, not merely reading good management books.

An authentic vision for progress doesn't just appear out of the ether, nor does it simply grow from what others believe to be important. Passion about what we want to change grows from the foundation of values that have been formed by our life experience. These values are vital to us personally, not because they are socially acceptable, not because they look good on a plaque on the wall (although both might be true), but because we have actually experienced them to be true.

Warren Bennis, who has studied leadership longer than any other American scholar, continues to stress the need for such self-knowledge for being effective as an agent of progress. When reflecting on his own performance as president of the University of Cincinnati, he found that when he was most effective it was because he knew what he wanted. It was that experience that drew Bennis to define the first competency of leadership as the *"management of attention."*[1] He continued to stress this need for focus on the delineation of individual values: "Anyone who wants to express himself fully and truly must have a point of view. Leadership without perspective and point of view isn't leadership—and of course it must be your own perspective, your own point of view. You cannot borrow a point of view any more than you can borrow someone else's eyes. It must be authentic, and if it is, it will be original, because you are an original."[2]

I'm dismayed by the number of men and women I interview who have retired from leadership positions decrying their failure to take time for personal reflection while they were active in their post. Even more, current clients also report a paucity of time to think, to ponder, to expand. This phenomenon is simply getting worse as electronic media demand attention 24/7. I've now adopted two principles of interviewing that I use to help a board decide on a new leader. Initially, I make it clear that I'm not looking for someone who is looking for a job or someone who is looking for more money. I'm looking for someone who has something to do in life and is looking for a place to do it. Then I ask, "What have you done, in the last twelve months, with your own money and on your own time, to develop your capability to lead?"

In general, people assume leadership positions in organizations that they did not found, and rather than initially considering the impact they might make on the organization and proceeding from a foundation of values, they define themselves as they go along. First they accept the old tenets of the organization, and only gradually, if ever, discover what is important to them personally. This trial-and-error method of leadership often results in an inconsistent message and a lack of commitment by those engaged in the enterprise.

Leaders who either make it clear that they have internalized the old set of dominant values or who gravitate the organization to a set that reflects their own beliefs make a substantial mark on the organization. Those who do not make their values clear become caretakers—and they are often replaced when the first significant challenge faces the enterprise. John Sculley successfully made this transition at Apple. His successors Michael Spindler and Gil Amelio did not. Spindler was to put the financial ship right, while Amelio was to lead Apple to a new vision. Unfortunately, Amelio seemed to have no idea what he wanted to do at Apple before he assumed the leadership of this deeply passionate company. By the time he started to communicate his ideas nearly a year had gone by, and nearly all of the early enthusiasm of a great number of dedicated people had drained out of the company. It took the re-ascendance of Steve Jobs, the spiritual leader of this firm, to right it.

Jobs had the secret of knowing who he was. Years later, in 2005, he was to reveal more specifics in a speech to the graduating class at Stanford. "I'm convinced," he said, "that the only thing that kept me going was that I loved what I did. You've got to find what you love."[3] Jobs was able to make the transition back into Apple because he loved that it stood for his values, not because it made money.

Lou Gerstner successfully made the transition at IBM. John Ackers, the previous CEO, did not. Gerstner changed IBM fundamentally—from a hardware company to a systems integrator and service company. Ackers, who had come from the same lineage as every other IBM CEO, could not conceive of such a fundamental transformation. Ronald Reagan and Bill Clinton successfully made the transition as president of the United States. The intervening president, George Bush Sr., did not. Although clearly a gracious and capable individual, he was "Reagan lite," and many people felt it.

Like Jobs, the successful leaders spoke frequently and effectively about their convictions. Former New York governor Mario Cuomo, arguably the best U.S. political communicator of the last three decades, reflects on his motivation to speak in his self-edited compendium *More Than Words*: "For me, the vital thing is that *there is something important I want to say*. . . . As I look back over the speeches I selected for this volume, I note that most of the things I was trying to say revolved around the *small cluster of basic ideas that have resonated with me for most of my adult life*" (emphasis mine).[4]

These core ideas (the rule of law, insistence on a sense of responsibility, the rejection of the melting pot for the mosaic view of our multiculturalism, the need for seeing our disparate society as a family, the belief that work is better than welfare, and the idea that economic growth is the provider of the American dream) were the topics for Cuomo's best-planned speeches, the ones he considers his most definitive. It's important to note that these principles formed the basis for his informal communication as well. They defined Cuomo as a leader. This is the primary function of a Personal Leadership Communication Guide. It has been described as "a biography with a purpose."

You too will find that a very few ideas constitute the core of your philosophy. These principles are more than a point of view; they are the tenets you believe to be vital to address, the questions that you wrestle with intellectually and emotionally, and they probably represent the quandaries of your personal life as well; perhaps in different dress, but the same nonetheless.

Delineating your point of view, then, is the first step toward communicating authentically. You don't have to write eloquent speeches, but you do have to develop and refine the message or messages that define you.

As you explore the creation of a Personal Leadership Communication Guide in the second half of the book, your fundamental values will be holding the pen. Simply put, a person who is not at least struggling with these questions of "Who are you?" and "What are you here to do?" just can't lead. Any message about significant change constructed without reflection on its importance to you personally will not inspire you, and will not, therefore, inspire others. To engage in the search for answers to these questions, you don't have to look far. The answers are inside you, sometimes eager to get out.

Recognizing and Reflecting on Your Point of View—Defining Moments

Every idea that you hold passionately has a background in your personal experience. Two of the bases of predictive psychology are first, that our beliefs are a product of our past teachings, and second, that those things learned through actual experience and personal observation have more power to form our future than ideas learned by abstract examination.

The personal nature of our life path has roots in ancient lore. The Greeks claimed that our life force is guided by *daimons* or attending spirits who define our destiny. Our daimon, believed the Greeks, invites us to certain life experiences and keeps us from others in order to further our development. The late James Hillman, the world's most noted archetypal psychologist, compared this daimon to similar beliefs in other traditions: "Hindus speak of karma; Romans would have called this ghost your genius. . . . In our century, [the concept] has reappeared as Jung's 'Wise Old Man' and 'Wise Old Woman,' who, Jung says, are 'configurations of the guiding Self.' "[5] According to the tradition of depth psychology, our life experiences, particularly trials that might result in neurosis, are not necessarily to be cured, but rather to serve as guideposts to our future. By contrast, much of the Freudian approach regards many of our most influential and powerful past experiences as occurrences to live down or recover from. In this view, neuroses are to be cured, not observed for meaning.

Certainly there are cases where recovery is needed; but our feelings, compassion, conviction, and dedication to study are strengthened by our entire past, both good and bad experiences. At the extreme, the most compassionate counselors are those who have themselves experienced tragedy, addiction, or poverty, and the strongest leaders are those who have experienced or personally witnessed the negative effects of the status quo and the subsequent transformative power of change.

Steve Jobs cited his three defining moments when he spoke to the Stanford graduating class—leaving school, getting fired, and being diagnosed with cancer—and suggested that only in retrospect he could see that they were connected by a thread of always doing what he loved—quite a revelation, considering that at least two of his three defining moments would normally be considered negative.

For three hundred years, therapists and spiritual healers have searched for their subjects' defining moments, whether through hypnosis, regression, or talking therapy. Without regard to the complexity of analysis, the process of remembering is simple, just as Jobs discovered. Reflect on what has actually influenced your behaviors and attitudes. Identify those specific life experiences that you remember as significant, and then identify the value associated with that experience. If done with honesty, this kind of exercise will lead you to the basis for your own leadership, the fundamentals of a defining message, perhaps even to the institution within which you want to lead.

Howard Schultz found himself, at seven years old, with a father who had broken his leg on the job and a mother who took in washing from others just to make ends meet. He saw that his father had been worn down by the system. He had gone from one job to another, never having health insurance, and when he got hurt, he didn't work, and the family didn't eat. Schultz grew up to found Starbucks, and later wrote about his response to his father's plight:

> Years later, that image of my father—slumped on the family couch, his leg in a cast, unable to work or earn money, and ground down by the world—is still burned into my mind. Looking back now, I have a lot of respect for my dad. He never finished high school, but he was an honest man who worked hard. . . .
>
> The day he died, of lung cancer, in January 1988, was the saddest of my life. He had no savings, no pension. More important, he had never attained fulfillment and dignity from work he found meaningful.
>
> As a kid, I never had any idea that I would one day head a company. But I knew in my heart that if I was ever in a position where I could make a difference, I wouldn't leave people behind.[6]

What value did Schultz generate from this experience? It was the value of never leaving anyone behind, of creating a real sense of community. Schultz grew up determined to craft a place that would nurture those who worked there. As a result of that value, he successfully lobbied the SEC to grant stock to part-time Starbucks employees. Walk into any Starbucks and ask the employee behind the counter if they like working there and why, and you will see the reflection of Howard Schultz's image of his father on that couch. Most feel included. Few feel left behind. On the basis of his principles, Schultz was able to re-emerge as CEO in 2009 and rebuild a floundering Starbucks back to even greater success.

Communicating Through the Prism of Your Values

Merely discovering what matters will not assure that you can communicate to inspire. When I ask my executive classes to identify leaders of any period who were the most effective at inspiring others, the lists are remarkably consistent. Nelson Mandela, Martin Luther King, Joan of Arc, John F. Kennedy, Margaret Thatcher, Abraham Lincoln, and Anwar Sadat are always on the list. Spiritual leaders are consistently mentioned as well: Gandhi, Mohammed, Jesus, Siddhartha.

What do these people have in common?

Without hesitation, the group responds with words like *passion, commitment,* and *self-knowledge.* Often they miss the obvious, that people in this rare group were willing and able to communicate with others using the raw material of their own conviction. Clearly, these leaders were courageous enough to communicate authentically from the basis of their real values, whether they were giving speeches, advocating a cause, writing memos, or conversing informally. Whatever the venue, their commitment came through. We use words like *destined* or *fated* to describe the strength of their conviction, yet each of us has that calling, some louder than others, some more cluttered with other noise; nonetheless, our daimon is not just beckoning us to life, it is calling us to express ourselves.

Distilling Values into Conviction

In my executive and graduate school classes in leadership communication, each participant spends a significant amount of time developing a single message. I ask them to choose their topic by answering these questions:

- Given your defining moments, and the values associated with them, what condition in your chosen industry would you change and how?

- What is the most important social issue we have to deal with as a community (world, nation, state, etc.)? How would you correct it?
- What causes and goals receive the time, treasure, and talent you devote to personal philanthropy?

Participants are required to have had some personal experience in the issue that will illustrate how they formed their position on the subject. At the end of the process, they develop a Personal Leadership Communication Guide.

Developing the Guide reveals some solid conviction. Additionally, executives and graduate students alike realize before the program's end that the topic questions are interlaced; that is, their *values* create their conviction, whether it is about the value itself or about one of the applications of the value in business or society. For example, one student, Rob Nicholson, chose to communicate about the preservation of the environment, imploring others to take steps toward conservation of natural resources. This is a fairly common topic in California, as many people are environmentally conscious, especially on university campuses, perhaps particularly so at UC Berkeley. Accordingly, it is difficult to move people to further action; they believe they are already doing enough.

But Rob was not a typical conceptual environmentalist. A native of Canada, he related his own personal experience of observing lakes near his hometown lose their fish population to acid rain. He quoted a space shuttle astronaut's observation that there were only two manmade landmarks visible from space . . . the Great Wall of China and a massive old-growth clear-cut in Rob's home province. He was highly credible, as he had studied environmental science as an undergraduate, and he made an authentic connection with his fellow students through his strong personal conviction—an outgrowth of his personal experience.

Rob could draw on his environmental experience to communicate metaphorically about business or political issues. The preservation of capital, the efficient use of by-products, the idea of personal responsibility for the greater good—these topics and others could be addressed using these same events to stimulate his own conviction. The strength of this message resulted from

Rob's reflection on a single question, and his use of the answer to develop the message. Today, fifteen years after developing that original Communication Guide, Rob is still involved in expressing those values. He is now in Toronto, having plied his talents in investment banking in San Francisco, New York, and indeed around the world. Many of his funded projects involve alternative energy, and his lifestyle and chosen location and company reflect his belief in collaboration and connection rather than competitive financial wrangling. In a recent conversation, Rob said that he realizes that he has done business with many of the same people through the years because he was able to develop lasting relationships and trust with them—another value that he revealed in his days at Berkeley.

Others too, interviewed in earlier editions and whose stories are updated in this edition, have found their Communication Guides useful in defining their life's work. In 2002, Josie Gaillard's Guide was a plea and a plan for energy independence for the United States. After gaining her MBA, she worked for a solar panel company, and now she and her husband are building an energy-neutral home; she owns and operates a virtual store, Living Ethos (www.livingethos.com), that offers eco-friendly gift wraps and other similar earth-friendly products. Rebekah Saul Butler expanded her class conviction about end-of-life decisions to a professional interest in the cost of health care, an issue she is engaged in as program director of a philanthropic foundation.

Whether you are a student, a rising executive, or a seasoned politician, contemplating your life story will often yield not just one but an array of individual values as well as their relative importance. Accordingly, I ask each corporate and political client to prepare an autobiography as a first step toward learning to communicate authentically. I request that they pay particular attention to events in their past that seem like turning points, events that have prompted fundamental decisions about the relative importance of ideas, things, and behaviors. We then use these events to construct complete Communication Guides around fundamental themes, drawing out their authentic concerns.

In late 1994, I worked with the executive team of a small company, Taylor-Made Office Systems, to help them redefine their vision and values. In the process I became close friends with

Barry Taylor, the founder and CEO, and discovered that he had been orphaned as a boy, started his business as a very young man, and delivered his product to customers from his own second-hand truck. In addition, he had been divorced twice and had tragically lost a teenage son in an accident. These events and his many specific vivid memories of them shaped his values.

Barry had grown his company to three hundred employees and nearly $150 million, but it still exemplified his basic values. Is it any wonder that he emphasizes a strong family feeling, independence, and the need to serve the customer above all else? To this entrepreneur, these values did not come from a quick read of popular management books, they came from his life, and they carried with them all the authenticity of his own passion and conviction.

Barry has since sold his original company, regrouped, and started two others with the same fundamental values at their core. In addition, he and his wife Elaine have funded and built a summer camp for kids with cancer—an outgrowth of his own childhood and the values that it formed.

Like Barry Taylor, Ed McDannell, Dave Gaisford, Mario Cuomo, Howard Schultz, Rob Nicholson, Steve Jobs, William Miller, Gary Fiedel, Rebekah Saul-Butler, Josie Gaillard, and every other leader who has led change effectively, each of us has something unique to say, and it is based on our particular makeup and our rich and sometimes dire experience. To communicate as an authentic leader, you have to look for your own daimon, look into your own experience, and find those themes that are most important to you.

***

The well of human experience is indeed deep. But the treasures are worth the effort of going into this water, especially if you want to have a conscious and meaningful impact on the world in which you live. You don't need to sit in a cave for twenty years; at least some of the treasure is accessible in your normal life's context. Once you discover the themes that matter most to you, you can convert them to inspiration for others—but only if you are courageous, disciplined, and emotionally attuned enough to do so.

Chapter Two

Deepening Emotional Awareness

Discovery and clarification of personal values does not, in itself, create good communication skills—nor does it guarantee the ability to lead.

To lead involves a substantially different decision than merely to get something done. Rather than deciding to lead, you could decide to become a good artist or a compelling author—someone who perhaps has great personal insight—an invaluable individual contributor who achieves outstanding results alone. Many philosophers contribute in this way, as do many of our most accomplished commentators.

In organizations, each of us can do exceptional work that expresses our values without communicating with others directly, and even when we do communicate, we can merely tell people what we need done to accomplish our own ends, or we can advise others on how to act. Some psychologists, many of our best business and political consultants, many managers, and certainly many of our best thinkers fall into this mode. It is important work—but it is not the same as leading. *Leading* is a personal pursuit that by definition does not merely use other people but involves them. The primary distinction between a leader and someone who merely conceives and expresses good ideas or examples, or who merely gets results, is the ability to relate to others in a way that inspires them.

While the logical mind is a great tool for gaining agreement, it is not sufficient to build strong bonds or to create commitment. Accordingly, a second internal necessity for integration into the

Personal Leadership Communication Guide is documenting your emotional awareness. Only in the last few years have we discovered that emotional capacity can be developed throughout life—our level of awareness and use of emotions is not fixed by our age, sex, the nature of our childhood, or our native culture. Your decision to lead requires you to become aware of this capacity and develop it.

Recognition, Resonance, Regulation, and Response

In 1995, Daniel Goleman made the case for emotional intelligence (E.I.) as fundamental to leadership. Since his pioneering work, many others have contributed to the research, some for a broader general audience, some focusing exclusively on leadership. This book explores both strains of E.I. work, but the discussion focuses through the lens of leadership communication. This is the subject that is most relevant as we are trying to engage people to be creative in the context of everyday work, when we are trying to work with others on teams, and when we are trying to set a vision, or define the pace and the nature of the work for any enterprise in a way that others are inspired.

In 2011, I had been facilitating some learning at Stanford for a group from Great Britain, and in the course of the day, I quoted from the original work of anthropologist Paul Ekman. Ekman, retired from the University of California, San Francisco, is still doing research and consulting on the phenomenon of reading facial cues to determine the emotional landscape of another person. He did his original field work to prove a thesis of Margaret Mead—that emotional facial expressions were formed by individual cultures—but he proved the opposite. People have an innate and universal ability to recognize emotion in others, says Ekman, and it is therefore not relative to a particular culture.[1] We are unconsciously aware of others' feelings, but through observation of facial expression and other anatomical cues, we can train ourselves to consciously determine the emotion of another person. This is one aspect of emotional intelligence.

Developing this capacity is easier than was thought only a few years ago. The value in doing so is significant in all venues, and particularly for those working in cross-cultural environments. It's important to note that the effort involves recognizing the unconscious, not learning a new skill from its root. The skills of E.I. flow from our common and inborn ability, and when activated will allow us to at least partially transcend barriers of language or particular cultural mores.

I had been unaware that Ekman was to be the evening speaker for the Stanford group, but through a couple of unlikely coincidences, I was able to meet with him privately for a few minutes before his presentation. What excites Ekman most is not just the universality of the facial cues that indicate emotion but our ability to actually develop greater awareness of those cues throughout our lifespan. As we attempt to be more discerning, our brains actually create new neural pathways, a process known as *neuroplasticity*. Enhancing E.I. is indeed possible—whatever your age or role—and the rewards are substantial.

Beyond mere *recognition* of the emotions in ourselves and in others, central aspects of E.I.—empathy (*resonance*), *regulation* of our internal process, and *responding* rather than reacting—can be developed throughout life as well. Science formerly postulated that the ability to relate emotionally was fixed by genetics and childhood environment, but it is now well documented that these traits can be altered by practice and neural feedback from new experiences.

The idea of E.I. seems experientially correct; few people ever make important decisions in life based on logic alone, and those who do frequently live with emotional regret. In the years since Goleman's work was first published, he and others have shown the science-based social neurobiological research that makes the importance of emotional intelligence credible, if not incontrovertible.

A General Theory of Love, by Thomas Lewis, Fari Amini, and Richard Lannon, clarifies and applies Goleman's work pertaining to limbic resonance and empathy.[2] For me, that book remains the most powerful exploration of the effect of early-life emotional attachment, the nature of empathy, and the challenge of shifting one's personality to be more understanding, trusting, and accepting. Its introduction to the limbic system of the brain and its responsibility for implicit or patterned memory is an eye-opener. Operating eighty thousand times faster than the thinking part of the brain, this emotional limbic lobe, through its messenger switch the amygdala, pushes us to *react* to emotional stimuli, much of the time before we know what we are doing. Hence, in situations that might be tense, we retort rather than respond, often with consequences we would not have chosen. In essence our consciousness is hijacked, and our natural empathy has no time to save us. Leaders are rarely made aware of their knee-jerk reactions. Instead, they are often left wondering about the lack of response or are surprised to receive adverse reactions to their spontaneous retorts.

In 2010, I was introduced to one of the general managers of a large U.S.-based multinational. He was charged with rebuilding a worldwide business in a technical field. During a Webex meeting with employees worldwide, he exhorted the group to continue to innovate and submit patent applications, because they were "the lifeblood of the business." After the presentation, a questioner from the south of the United States posed a question: "We just got a memo from someone on the corporate staff telling us that the company was not going to spend as much money defending patents. How does that square with your comment about the importance of continuing to invent?"

With no hesitation, the general manager said, "The corporate staff doesn't run the business, we do!" This, of course, drew a loud round of applause from the group, and shortly thereafter, the meeting was brought to a close.

In the aftermath, the client and I had a discussion of the impact of his answer and possible alternatives. Clearly, his amygdala had hijacked his response and turned it into a reaction. His is a wonderfully managed company with a cultural norm of working together across divisions. My client was one of three general managers, and they all had a close relationship with the CEO and the corporate staff. This incident also happened in a time of austerity—everyone was trying to conserve money.

There was little doubt that my client's comment was going to get back to the author of the corporate memo. As a consequence, my client might have had a tarnished reputation, might be characterized as a tyrant or a prima donna, and might be thought to have blamed someone not connected to the business as a whole. He had also given his entire business unit a rebellious message about the corporate staff. What could he have said that would have both satisfied the questioner and sent the right message to all involved?

Together, we decided he could have tried this:

> You know, I don't know why that kind of memo would have been written, but I can imagine. We are all looking for ways to save money, and I would bet that the author found an opportunity somewhere in the volume of fees that are charged to sustain patents that are old. There are probably thousands of patents that are outdated and no longer represent a competitive advantage for our firm. It would be senseless to continue to spend money to defend them, just as it would be senseless to stop supporting new work that gives us a technical lead in our markets. I suspect that memo reflects that kind of decision, which, by the way, I would applaud, just as I would applaud any one of our partners on the corporate staff who is consciously looking for ways to lower expenses so that we can invest where it counts. If the answer is any different, I will get back to you, but I can assure you that we are being very aggressive about generating and defending patents that matter.

Naturally, this reasoned empathic response is much easier to conceive after the original rush of adrenaline, the assault on the amygdala, and the rapid-fire action of the limbic brain. It is possible to train ourselves to make this adjustment in the moment, but it does require recognition and regulation, the results of awareness and practice. In this situation, my client could have been instantly aware (recognition) that he was in emotional mode (peeved, upset, surprised), taken stock of that fact for just a moment (it takes only two hundred milliseconds to react), considered how the asker of the question and the writer of the memo must have been feeling (resonance and empathy), tempered his own emotion (regulation), and responded rather than reacted. We know now that this is possible and, in fact, we are trained in these skills from early childhood, typically without any direct awareness. How do we consciously transmit recognition, resonance, regulation, and response?

Monks are great at this patient, thoughtful response—through practice. Imagine, for example, a monk sitting in meditation while the person beside him is snoring. The monk might first sit in meditation and watch his own irritation at the person snoring. Instead of allowing that irritation to grow, the monk then puts his mind into a state of loving-kindness, accepting that the person with whom he is irritated probably hasn't slept in days, came to the retreat in a state of complete disarray, and therefore deserves his understanding. Then he regulates his own emotions, extending consideration (and, in an advanced form, even love), and at the end of the meditation extends an invitation to dinner. Ah, if we could just translate this ideal response to the internal and external world in which most of us live every single day. Science offers some suggestions that may help.

The Neurobiology of Empathy: The Magic of the Mirror

The first research regarding the nature and neurological source of empathy was done by Giacomo Rizzolatti and his colleagues in the early 1990s in Parma, Italy. Using monkeys as subjects and physical probes to the brain as data gatherers, they discovered that the same neurons were activated when a subject monkey performed a certain task himself and when he merely watched another monkey doing the same task. It seemed that the brain of the watching monkey was *mirroring* that of the doing monkey.

The implications were profound. It seemed that imitation of others was the default way of learning. For baby mammals, including humans, this seems natural. If the mother smiles at the baby, the baby eventually smiles back. The baby's brain is creating a model, a mirror, of the mother's brain; the baby learns to act in a certain way, and by mirroring well, both get more positive feedback.

Empathy in Humans

To expound on the new research extensively would require many volumes in itself, so I can only present comments here—not meant to be inclusive but rather representative, instructive, and hopefully encouraging. For those who want to dig into this fascinating and perhaps life-changing research and the corresponding possibilities of personal progress, I have included more references in the recommended reading list. Right now the interesting point is how to apply the conclusions of this science to the ability to communicate in a way that inspires others.

Since the inception of the technology of functional magnetic resonance imaging (fMRI), researchers have been able to identify, without invasive probes, neurons that are active in the human brain when certain stimuli occur, thus allowing us to rapidly gain understanding about the brain's particular sectors that control our sense of self and of others without relying on extrapolation from tests on other animals. In particular, we have expanded our understanding of how humans learn social behavior—largely through imitation—facilitated by these same mirror neurons in the brain. Now, through the work of researchers including Richard Davidson, Dan Seigel, Matthew Lieberman, and Marco Iacaboni, we have learned that while the mirror neuron mechanism involves a slightly different progression in adults, the process continues for life—we learn and can actually develop new neurons to facilitate that learning. Depending on the level of our attention, not only do we fire neurons that would be activated if we were doing the task, but neurons fire that would create in us the same emotional response that the doer would be experiencing. *Empathy* is so defined: "The power of projecting one's personality into (and so fully comprehending) the object of contemplation."

But as adults, our superactive cerebral cortexes inhibit our ability to empathize, as the noise level of reasoning often drowns out our ability to consciously notice how others are feeling. The more we value our ability to reason, the less we can access our emotions.

While the science of emotional and social neurobiology moves forward, what perhaps hasn't been fully acknowledged is the hard work it takes to make even slight movements in consciousness and awareness, to do more than merely go through the motions. What Goleman and Lannon call "resonance" is not just "being on the same page" intellectually, it is being in the same zone emotionally, sharing the same dreams, hoping for the same outcomes, disclosing the feelings of risk, communicating about joy, fear, hope, and frustration, even love. Nowhere is this skill more demonstrable than in our personal relationships. The stakes are often high, and we'd be wise to pay a bit more attention.

When I was divorced in 1982, I was fortunate to be awarded full physical custody of my two sons, even as my five-year-old daughter was leaving to live with her mother in a different city. The boys were thirteen and eleven at the time, and over the next few years, we three learned the importance of being emotionally honest with ourselves and one another. I can vividly remember one of my sons packing his things in his room and telling me that he was moving out, either to go live with a friend or to go to his mom's house some fifty miles away. While the disagreement between us had been over something substantive, I realized, given his strong will, that he would probably go, and would never be able to return, even if it were the obvious and right thing to do. As he stood there with a small bag packed, a part of me wanted to send him on his way and tell him that he would regret it. But as emotion welled up in me, as the possibility of his leaving became real, I was able to tell him that while we had had a disagreement, and while I was angry, as he was, we would have to work it out. I told him that I really didn't want him to leave, that I loved him, and that despite still being angry, I was also afraid that we were doing the wrong thing. I did not want to lose my special connection with him.

He stayed, actually admitting that he didn't want to lose the connection either. This was not the only "learning opportunity" in the next few years. Through a series of interactions such as this one, all three of us discovered and began to more fully appreciate the importance of giving voice to our emotions.

As leaders, we have followers and constituents who are rarely our children. But because *all* relationships are forged through communication, spoken and unspoken, we must add this skill of emotional relating to our repertoire when we lead, practicing recognition, resonance, regulation, and response both in the moment and as we plan our communication guides for change.

To see these phenomena in action on the screen, watch the black-and-white rendition of *Twelve Angry Men.*[3] In the story, Henry Fonda's character convinces his eleven peers to change their guilty votes by carefully noticing and then relating the likely emotional landscape of the players, from the prosecutor and defense attorney to the defendant, the witnesses—even the murder victim himself. Seen through this lens, his character becomes more than a debater or the most persuasive of the jurors, he displays the very nature of empathy from the beginning of the trial to the end.

Retorts in the moment typically provide the biggest challenge to emotional engagement. In developing our own Communication Guide, we can take the time to anticipate how others will react emotionally, imagine how we might react ourselves, and plan accordingly. At the same time, we are beginning to train ourselves to respond rather than react to inevitable challenges. Disclosure of our own emotions and acknowledging those of the people we hope to engage is a practice that is now widely recognized as a core competence of leading, and our specific reflections should be included in the Guide.

In the earlier example concerning patents, my client needed to buy time, while waiting for his brain function to shift from the limbic system to the cortex. Buying time is not merely taking a deep breath before you lay into someone. It is applying your new knowledge about what is going on in your brain and in others' brains that will need regulating with communication. Imagining the feelings of the other person and verbalizing them with understanding is an ideal way to purchase a moment.

Showing the Math

You'll notice that my client's "preferred response" was based on imagining why the corporate memo might have been written and then verbalizing that imagination. Judith Honesty, a former colleague at BlessingWhite, calls this process "showing the math." Those who took mathematics from algebra on up know the accuracy of the metaphor. By showing the actual work in a problem, rather than just the answer, students receive partial credit for their efforts, even if they did not get the right solution to the problem. In the same way, by revealing that inside emotional conversation, or the process of "getting the answer" about other problems, we earn partial credit, or credibility, or trust, from the listener, even if we are awkward in expressing it, or even if the listener thinks we have the wrong answer.

Transmitting Empathy to Show Character: Developing Trust

Using the imagination, practicing empathy, and "showing the math" are solid building blocks of trust. Thanks to Scott Adams (creator of "Dilbert") and the new speed of travel of some well-founded cynicism about leadership, trust is no longer the default response from constituents to those with authority, particularly in business and politics. When "Dilbert" was beginning to bloom in every cubicle in the United States, the Internet was giving us opportunities to develop, post to, and search sites where one could offer comments, totally uncensored, about one's leader or anything else.

The proliferation of social media makes it possible for anyone to make a comment about anything, complementary or otherwise. Add this to the hounding nature of a public media that is voracious for any news at all, and the general capability to broadcast opinions without fact-checking, and you have a daunting force capable of undermining trust. How does a leader maintain any semblance of trustworthiness without an army of spin artists and a fortress of privacy? One answer, which may seem intimidating, is to use your imagination and verbalize your empathy. One of the world's best companies gave us a prime example of what happens when a leader doesn't do that.

The earliest large-scale debacle occasioned by the new speed of revelation was Intel's failure to acknowledge a default in a Pentium chip, a failure that, according to technology reporter Vince Emery, "cost the company millions of dollars and could easily have been prevented."[4] The irony of Intel falling victim to its own technology is easy to appreciate. This particular chip had limited application, and the problem caused an error in the fifteenth decimal place. The Intel engineers decided that few customers would encounter the problem, and Intel's chief executive decided that rather than disclosing the flaw and replacing chips found to be defective, Intel would wait for customers to complain and replace the units individually.

Intel's engineers discovered the error in June 1994. By November of that year, Intel had become a laughing stock on the Internet. Andy Grove, president of Intel, chose to post a message on an Internet newsgroup trying to mitigate what was now a public relations disaster. Grove's message was not posted from his own address, so many readers, according to Emery, believed it was a spoof. It bore no return address, was generic, and communicated little regret.[5] Only three short sentences into the message, the writer says, "Let me give you my perspective on what has happened here."[6]

Jokes began to appear: "At Intel, quality is job .999999998," and "The Intel version of *Casablanca:* 'Round off the usual suspects.'"

What could Intel and Grove have done? With hindsight, it seems obvious. The very chip they were producing is what allowed the flaw to be publicized, their company to be ridiculed, and—perhaps the worst results—a loss of belief in the character of the company and a loss of trust in its president. Grove could have gone public immediately, acknowledged the mistake, and offered to replace the chips.

It's easy enough to analyze why that was not his course of action—especially with the benefit of looking back at a disaster. In truth, the problem was indeed significant to only a small number of Intel's customers. The issue was not the error's impact but the lack of understanding and empathy (and therefore a question about the character of Intel and its leadership). The problem was 5 percent objective and 95 percent emotional. The lesson? Recognize the emotions of those impacted by your action, resonate with them, regulate your own emotions, and then respond. This disaster could have been averted, and indeed could have been used to build loyalty. Leadership failed to understand, and therefore failed to respond in a positive way. The act of making an internal conversation external will make it possible to defuse many disagreements over time, and can even heal old wounds.

When it counts most, we can do this. Personally, a willingness and ability to show the math made it possible to reconcile with my daughter, who had been distant, had perhaps felt left out, and who had naturally been influenced by being essentially separate. At a restaurant in Petaluma, she and I had one pivotal conversation in which we both stopped pretending not to be hurt, and showed the math. After nearly twenty years of being cordial with one another, real love had a place to show up. And it did.

Leadership: Empathy in Action

However you wish to express it, empathy is necessary for leadership. Richard Davidson, professor of psychology and psychiatry at University of Wisconsin, divides emotional propensities into emotional styles. With regard to social intuition, he says, "Leaders and teachers need to be sensitive to the cues of those around them . . . [and] sensitive to the niceties of the social environment to respond appropriately in a given situation."[7] Ignoring feelings and using intimidation can work for a while to accomplish tasks, but not to inspire real contribution, especially in today's creativity-driven environment, and this distinction has been active for a while.

What does this have to do with leadership? Everything.

In the mid-nineties, I was coaching a top-level executive who had as much potential as anyone I had met. His track record of getting results was sterling; it included assuming responsibility for three very large operations in three very large companies, all within a seven-year period. He had international experience and an advanced degree from a prestigious university. He was one of the smartest, quickest people I had encountered. He also had one of the highest needs of anyone I had met to satisfy his enormous ego, and he demonstrated no empathy or appreciation for others.

Unfortunately, his communication reflected his hubris. The only emotions he could express at work were frustration, impatience, and anger. Rather than acknowledging these as signs of his own drive to succeed that might need modification as he gained more responsibility, he spewed them out indiscriminately in increasingly heavy doses to those who worked for him. At the zenith of his career, he was responsible for nearly 70 percent of the operations and 80 percent of the people in the company. His default was to engender fear, not hope; insecurity, not confidence.

In the short term, the results of his group were excellent. They exceeded even the most optimistic forecasts of the strategists. In the wake of his short-term success, he was hoping to be promoted to run the company, and as a step toward that possibility, asked for some feedback on his ability to lead. A colleague administered a 360-degree feedback instrument to the executive's direct reports. The results were predictable. While this executive was at the top of the "competence" ranking, he was at the bottom of the "connection" ranking. His style of communicating not only engendered fear in those who encountered him, it was also demoralizing many of his charges.

In the debrief of the responses to the instrument, the executive asked the right question: "Do I have to change to be successful?" My colleague and I replied almost simultaneously, "No, unless you want to stay here." He did not change, but left under duress shortly thereafter, totally unable to take advantage of his exceptional knowledge of the business and his ability to hold people accountable because of his inability to engender trust. He went on to start another enterprise that skyrocketed in the beginning and died when it needed energy from others to continue to grow.

This profile is not unusual for turnaround specialists in sports, business, or politics. When operations are in disarray, intimidation from a strict no-nonsense autocrat can indeed turn people's attention sharply to their responsibilities. But this intense pressure for accountability isn't enough to sustain success for the long term. Only in recognizing and acknowledging our own feelings can we recognize and acknowledge others' feelings. And only then can a leader develop the bond of trust necessary for commitment and continued contribution.

Managing Your Emotional Response

Strong feelings are of course common in the world of leading change. If leaders recognize their own automatic emotional responses, they can adjust their communication to be more appropriate, less damaging, more inspiring.

David Pottruck, friend, former client, and former CEO of Charles Schwab Corporation, reported an example of the need for emotional intelligence in *Clicks and Mortar.*

> Earlier in 1999, I spoke to a conference of Wall Street analysts interested in the financial services industry. The speaker just before me in the program was an analyst with an expertise in electronic commerce. He commented during his remarks that the competition for electronic commerce in our industry was

> essentially over, that the discount brokerages had won, and that the banks were "losers." I was the next speaker, and as I promised my host, I spoke about Schwab's expansion on the Internet as well as some recent new business ventures that we had tried, including clearing mutual fund transactions for third parties and offering term life insurance. During the question and answer period that followed, one participant asked me if "Schwab would become a bank." I immediately quipped, "Why would we want to become a loser?
>
> Now, I made the remark as a joke, and it did get a laugh, but even as it was coming out of my mouth, I was picturing it as a headline, printed by a reporter who was in the room. I went on to answer the question more completely, and after the session, found the reporter. I told him that I realized how my "witty comment" would look quoted out of context, and that I clearly shouldn't have made the comment. He was gracious, said that he understood, and did not print the quip. But in the interchange and in my own reminder to myself, I learned again the care with which a leader has to comport himself.[8]

What Dave did not report in his account was a later conversation he had with the communications group at Schwab. The chief communication officer was trying to explain the lesson to the group and concluded by saying, "Watch what you say in front of reporters." Dave added the following comment: "Yes," he said, "it is certainly important to watch what we say in front of reporters, but the real reason I shouldn't have made that comment has nothing to do with the press. I shouldn't have made that comment because anyone who heard me refer to someone else or some group as 'losers' would assume I was capable of saying that about them when they were not listening. If I feel that way, I need to be aware of it, so that I can manage that response in myself and build my own character."

Dave's response shows the link between empathy and character that Goleman and others refer to:

> There is growing evidence that fundamental ethical stances in life stem from underlying emotional capacities. . . . For one, impulse is the medium of emotion; the seed of all impulse is a feeling bursting to express itself in action. Those at the mercy

> of impulse . . . who lack self-control . . . suffer a moral deficiency. The ability to control impulse is the base of will and character. By the same token, the root of altruism lies in empathy, the ability to read emotions in others; lacking a sense of another's need or despair, there is no caring.[9]

Certainly, anyone who watched the 2002 testimony of Enron executives before the U.S. Congress saw a dearth of emotional expression from these apparently intelligent men and women, similar to the 1998 testimony of the tobacco executives who all stood and affirmed that they did not believe that smoking cigarettes caused cancer. Add to this the more recent testimony of Wall Street executives who had plundered the financial system by packaging and marketing derivatives of fundamentally unredeemable mortgages. These outwardly unfeeling, uncaring leaders were not only bereft of much self-knowledge, they were apparently empty of empathy. Few showed any remorse, much less any responsibility. It would be easy to conclude that they were short on character as well.

Becoming Aware and Wary of Self-Importance

Understanding our own emotions and developing empathy toward others also exposes our own egos and our individual need for recognition. Everyone wants to be recognized, but Jim Collins, in his research on leadership that brought companies from good to great, emphasizes this aspect of leadership: "Leadership is about creating a climate where the truth is heard and the brutal facts confronted. There's a huge difference between the opportunity to 'have your say' and opportunity to be heard. The good-to-great leaders understood this distinction, creating a culture wherein people had a tremendous opportunity to be heard and, ultimately, for the truth to be heard."[10]

Being able to create this kind of climate requires a high degree of emotional intelligence, and a willingness to give up the central role of hero or heroine in the organization.

In the year 2000, Tom Murphy was chief information officer of Royal Caribbean Cruises Ltd. in Miami, Florida. He had enjoyed a meteoric career and had jumped from job to job fixing troubled organizations. He came to RCCL in 1999 after successful stints at Marriott and Omni Hotels, where he had been the youngest officer at both companies. In these and other organizations, he had quickly turned bad situations around and then left for another opportunity. He started at RCCL in the same way. He rapidly assessed the IT team, reorganized, and began to get results. They won Department of the Year in 1999, consecutive Best Places to Work in IT awards in 2000 and 2001, and multiple honors for innovation and web excellence.

Unlike many turnaround specialists, Tom was not an emotional cripple. He had a gregarious personality, and approached his job with passion and commitment to exceeding customer expectations. But as he later realized, the focus was always on him. In early 2001, he partnered with his organizational specialist to get the team some leadership training. I met him at the first session of an executive course in values clarification, leadership, and culture building in the Miami offices of the company.

Because the course was designed to bring a team together around some principles, maximizing its benefit required a great deal of emotional intelligence from the participants. They were asked to be vulnerable, and also to hold each other accountable for honest communication about problems in the organization.

Tom demonstrated a quick wit and with it a sharp tongue, and yet had the capacity to goad others on to greater participation than they would otherwise have been capable of. While I liked him immensely and felt that he had substantial talent and energy, I noticed that he managed to maintain the intellectual respect of the group, and that he also stayed on the outside, not really engaging personally.

This is what Tom told me about the effect of his experience in the training:

> My style, called a lightning rod or "Organizational Identification" by Harvard's Abraham Zaleznik, helped IT to overcome strong negative perceptions on the part of the business and strong internal challenges from early on. There is power in getting people to identify with you so strongly that you become a constant presence in their thinking. When you become an object of identification to your team, when you

> allow them to use you like that, the result is enormous cohesion. . . . There is a contagious power to this identification and it creates a singular focus throughout the organization.
>
> What I didn't realize at the time was that this approach has unseen ramifications that can negatively impact the leadership team, management group, and IT's overall performance over time. If the group becomes overly reliant on a single source for energy, passion, and vision, where does it go when that source is no longer available? . . . My history of moving from job to job was well known and . . . I felt a sort of perverse sense of pride that came when a former organization started to falter after I had left.

As a result of this realization, Tom made a decision to stay at RCCL and work to develop the people who worked with him. In making that commitment to his team, he was able to become more authentic in his communication, and, in his words, "discuss issues that we would not have otherwise discussed." He adds, "As we started dealing with one another on a different level, our trust grew. We were drawn closer to each other at a personal level as well." It was by exercising emotional intelligence that he made a major step forward in leadership.

After his tenure at Royal Caribbean, Tom was chosen to lead a substantial transformation at AmerisourceBergen Corporation in Pennsylvania. The project involved outsourcing and completely transforming the distribution systems to keep ABC competitively positioned. Tom said it was the hardest thing he ever did. He brought some lieutenants with him from RCCL, hired new expertise in his inner circle, and continued to try to develop others to take responsibility. He laid back in board meetings, allowing others to present, just as he had in his previous position.

Not every story has a happy ending. Tom left ABC when the transformation was nearly complete, but he believes that had he not chosen the inclusive means of leading, had he continued to be the lightning rod, he might have been more personally successful in the eyes of senior executives. It's true that some leaders see empathy, understanding, and inspiration as signs of weakness, but as Tom and I reviewed the results of his eleven-year effort, he was convinced that the project was too big and complex to be led by anyone focused solely on deadlines and measurements. His awareness and empathy were as important as his skill in large-scale IT in inspiring his team to excel.

Good leaders get people to work for them. Great leaders get people to work for a cause that is greater than any of them—and then for one another in service of that cause. By shifting the focus of his leadership, adopting the practice of introspection and authenticity, Tom has delivered more than results. He has delivered a group of people who want to struggle together to accomplish something none could do alone.

Tom's story is one of "discovering what matters" and "deepening emotional awareness": recognizing who he is, being appropriately vulnerable, emotionally resonating with others, regulating his process, and responding rather than reacting. People come to this kind of learning individually and—as I've personally discovered—sometimes with great effort. Some learn earlier than others, usually because their crucible is hotter, their experience more intense.

In 2000, I met Joe DeCola, a producer of *The Today Show* at NBC. I thought the meeting was about some potential book publicity, but it turned out to be about my own education. As we chatted about the attributes of authenticity, Joe told me of his eighteen-year-old daughter, Rebecca. She was then about to be a freshman at Oberlin, and had graduated from The Buxton School, a small private high school in Williamstown, Massachusetts. It was the brilliantly conceived ritual of the school to have each graduating senior give a short talk at graduation about what had informed their lives.

I should fill in some context. Joe and his former wife were very active in the political movements of the sixties, separated in the eighties when Rebecca was young, and kept a healthy relationship in her parenting. That's no small feat for any couple, but they managed all this even as Joe began to openly identify himself as homosexual.

He was clearly proud of Rebecca's graduation speech. I asked him for a copy, almost gratuitously, and he obliged. With my first reading, I laid it on my desk as tears welled up. I included the full text in the second edition of this book and I have received more inquiries about her progress than any other reported episode. I again include her statement of who she was and hoped to become. Her graduation speech is a premier example of expanding self-knowledge and emotional intelligence. Such maturation transforms the response that one might have to others who may—or may not—agree with them. It is reprinted again with Rebecca's permission:

> When I was small, I got to be in marches. I marched for abortion rights, equal rights for women, gay pride, AIDS funding. I went to folk concerts with my mother to raise money for the hungry, I worked at shelters to give soup to the homeless and I got to throw pink glittery Fairy Dust at angry people who said that my father and Adam and Steve would all burn in Hell.
>
> When I was a little larger, I was part of an environmental action committee and yelled about Styrofoam and recycling. I collected books, clothes, canned foods for people in Rwanda, New York and Kosovo. I volunteered over the summer for the Mohawk, and worked with the mentally ill. I raised money for Mumia and tried my darndest to not support corporate greed. I boycotted the Gap, Domino's, Exxon, Shell, Home Depot. I went hiking a lot, and I know about things like minimum impact and sustainable living. I have farmed for organic self-sufficient farmers, driven an efficient car across the country, and written letters protesting against logging, sweatshops, apartheid, hate crimes, prison systems, toxin dumping, the death penalty, and commercial fish trolling.
>
> These actions are important. They are valid and valiant and real. They are also part of being a little kid and being able to say that Barbies are bad for women, and your parents are Democrats, and you wear purple so you're okay. They made me feel aware, empowered, and moral. They made up a set of understandings which fit comfortably into a liberal sense of self. I do not have this sense anymore. I still think that there are some things that are just simply good, or simply unjust, but the list is getting increasingly smaller. The issues are much more blurred, the questions far too large for me to answer. I have realized recently that it is more and more difficult to make any STATEMENTS.

> I take much longer pauses before I say things and there are fewer and fewer T-Shirts that express what I am trying to say.
>
> I have come into a sense of my own ignorance and naïveté, which is both exciting and paralyzing. On one hand, it means that I want to learn more. I want to become more educated, and in doing this I will be able to affect things truly powerfully and precisely.
>
> On the other hand, it means I have lost the ability to just act. To directly confront things in that romantic raging way I thought I always could. I am more cautious, more fearful. I feel less sure of myself, and in losing the sense that there is some immutable solid truth out there, I lose my sense of when and how to act.
>
> Simply, the world is a complex, confusing place. It has taken me eighteen years to realize this in some of its entirety. I am trying to reconcile this understanding with the fact that I want to engage. I am trying to define my place in all of it. I don't want to simplify my life; I don't want to follow some guru's ten easy steps to happiness. I want to eat cheese and be honest. I don't want to be lost in idealistic adoration for this or that cause or this or that righteous leader, but I also don't want to throw my hands up and see everything with the grownup club's discussing-the-ills-of-the-world-over-latte distance. I want to really know what I am talking about before I start yelling.

This is not printed as an advocacy for any particular point of view, but rather as a demonstration of the growth that is necessary to develop the emotional intelligence to lead. Rebecca, at eighteen, was beginning to recognize the broad range of possible emotional responses and proclivities in others and giving up on her youthful conviction that she was always right. She was starting to see the shades of reality rather than only the sharp relief of her own point of view and emotions.

Not surprisingly, she has followed her eighteen-year-old convictions. She went on to graduate from Oberlin, briefly considered an academic career, then took a four-year post at her alma mater, Buxton School, where she taught ninth and twelfth grades and worked with graduating seniors on their personal college application essays, helping the students reflect their beliefs in their writing. She then moved to New York to get back to her family, and became a New York teaching fellow. She is completing a master's in Urban Adolescent Special Education at the same time she teaches full-time at the Lyons Community School in Brooklyn. Rebecca sings the praises of her mentor Taeko Onishi, a co-director of the school for inclusive leadership, who is always focused on kids who have not had economic advantages. Rebecca, Taeko, and the entire faculty will need all of their wonderful emotionally intelligent characteristics to support kids to succeed in this environment.

When I asked Rebecca if she ever wanted a role in public policy she said no—for the same reason she eschewed academic research. "I can never imagine myself spending all of my time talking to other adults about what should be done. I'd rather be doing it. I'd rather be keeping my focus on the reality of other people's lives and working toward changes."

***

Building this emotionally intelligent aspect of communication into your fundamental message will shift your good idea to a foundation for your inspirational interaction with others. The decision to lead has to include a decision to get to know your emotional makeup, recognize and respect emotions when they arise, communicate them responsibly, and develop the empathy necessary to relate to others on this same plane. These are topics for the next chapter, which takes up which communication tools facilitate emotional connections.

Chapter Three

Connecting with Others

The emotions have a major impact on our willingness to engage, to commit, to develop loyalty and trust. In fact, in addition to the real and constant need for operational excellence, the ability to connect emotionally is synonymous with leadership. Your achievement as a leader is measured in the success of others. The question is, How does a leader communicate material that will connect with the emotions, allowing others to link the more objective material—facts, data, logical arguments—with their psychic impulse, the fountain from which true inspiration flows? This process will also connect you to yourself. "To inspire," literally means "to breathe life into." This is difficult to do if you do not have the life in yourself.

Rebecca DeCola, whose graduation speech ended the preceding chapter, was, at eighteen, discovering how to access this interior impulse—to come to terms with her beliefs and learn how to relate to others in new and different ways—not to always oppose, not to ever appease, but to consider knowledge that might not be simplistic and relationships that form from complexity. How she pursued that exploration and applied what she learned would determine her ability to connect with others, to engage with them to find and create progress.

This same dynamic is at work in our best leaders all the time, even when they are dealing with the thorniest of issues. Consider abortion and access to abortion. Most would agree that use of abortion should be rare, yet proponents and opponents would disagree on the means to realize rarity in the practice. The issue becomes difficult, not because of some lack of reverence for life by those on either side of the issue, but because of the myriad other competing emotional and physical dynamics. This same quandary, the lack of simplicity that Rebecca was recognizing in her personal outlook, is true for nearly every change that is advocated by anyone who expresses values such as fairness, integrity, growth, survival, self-responsibility, loyalty, or community that we strive for in our own lives. We all grasp their importance, but the application of these values gets complicated and contentious—and demands the very best in our awareness and communication to accomplish anything significant.

Naturally, people have different views on how these values can best be expressed—as Rebecca was beginning to realize. How, then, do we reach a ground in our advocacy that will encourage everyone in the discussion to go beyond the parsing of details to arrive at the true values involved, and still incorporate facts? How can we connect in such a way that we respect one another's intention and integrity even as we struggle with the details? The conclusions will be grist for your Communication Guide.

Unconscious and Unspoken Harmonies

To begin to answer these thorny questions, it is useful to turn again to what science has learned and elaborated on since the turn of the new century. Today's research on the brain and its functions as mediator and guardian reveals expanded possibilities. Nearly all researchers agree that the old triune model of the brain is far too simplistic. Nonetheless, describing the functions of the brain in an evolutionary fashion remains a useful prototype and source of nomenclature.

While the reptilian stem of the human brain gives us impulses to fight or flee and the cortex gives us the ability to reason and decide, the workhorse of the system, the limbic brain, is receiving, interpreting, and routing data from conscious and unconscious systems. The limbic system acts as the creator of implicit memory—that which depends on similar patterns in our past to make snap decisions based primarily on emotional stimuli.

This marvelous arbiter of sensations processes up to ten million bits of input per second. It doesn't process abstract ideas;

it processes images, sounds, smells, narrative, and other subtle subjective and sensory information, compares those to past experience resident in implicit memory in these same forms—images, patterns, story, sounds, and other sensory data. It sends signals to the appropriate neural switches and then monitors the resulting emotions. This capability of the limbic brain allows us to make unconscious judgments about the trustworthiness of others and perhaps even to sense the meaning behind activities that are going on around us, to sense them before we are consciously aware of them. Through this system, we get into synch with other human beings, a capability referred to as "limbic resonance."[1]

Simply put, limbic resonance is what we call "connection," the magic sense of another's state and intention, and our corresponding relationship to them, whether it is signaled by feelings of dread or feelings of mutual attraction. It is this resonance that makes our experience of someone else a deeper experience than merely seeing two biologically similar eyes. In their marvelous work on the physiology of love, Thomas Lewis and his colleagues testify: "To the animals capable of bridging the gap between minds, limbic resonance supplies the wordless harmony we see everywhere but take for granted—between mother and infant, between a boy and his dog, between lovers holding hands across a restaurant table."[2] And I would add, between leaders and those they would inspire.

This is not an on-off system that we use selectively. It is operating unconsciously all the time, scanning the environment for attractions and dangers. Because of this capability, we are either attracted or repelled by others who look like, feel like, or sound like our parents or others who were significant in our maturation. Even more subtly, as noted in Chapter Two, we sense others' emotion and intention, even if they are not from our culture. Depending on our subtle interpretation, we will either be drawn to or repelled by potential spouses, by potential friends, by potential coworkers, and by potential leaders.

So as a leader, how do you cope with all of this subtlety? After all, you need to get things done! Annie Murphy Paul provided a quick introduction in her *New York Times* article "Your Brain on Fiction" in March 2012, reducing the stimulators of the limbic system to *language,* that medium in which leaders work. For example, she concludes from the research, "Stories . . . stimulate the brain and even change how we act in life."[3] This seems obvious, but the research goes deeper into the components of the stories to which we listen. Depending on our choice of words, particularly their sensory richness, very specific parts of the brain are activated. For example, "words like 'lavender,' 'cinnamon' and 'soap' . . . elicit a response not only from the language-processing areas of our brains, but also those devoted to dealing with smells."[4] These areas draw a far richer response than merely objectively seen words like *chair* or *key*.

Metaphors, too, when they refer to texture and touch rather than mere description, draw a response from the sensory cortex. Finally, just as with the mirror neuron system described in Chapter Two, the brain does not seem to make much distinction between reading or hearing about an experience and encountering it in real life. In each case, the same neurological regions are stimulated. Paul quotes Keith Oatley of the University of Toronto as saying, "A story goes beyond stimulating reality to give . . . the opportunity to enter fully into other people's thoughts and feelings."

As you begin to develop your Communication Guide, you need to look at the specific ways of communicating that appeal to this limbic brain, to that part of the mind that doesn't make distinctions or judgments, but rather connects with the other holistically. Focus on forms and language that will help you express your subjective Self, rather than merely your objective knowledge. Image, symbol, analogy, metaphor, story, myth, and the emotional component of personal experience are the tools of this type of communication. Each of these is distinct in appeal as well as function.

Image and Symbol

Image and symbol are best discussed together as they are often confused. An image can be a symbol, but it doesn't have to be. As Carl Jung explains, images "*stand* for things—they *name* things, but do *no more* than denote the objects to which they are attached."[5] Pictures of machinery, your group, or your house fall into this category. "A symbol conversely can be a term, a name, or even a picture that may be familiar in everyday life, yet it also possesses specific *connotations* in addition to its conventional and obvious (objective) meaning. It *implies* something vague, unknown, or hidden from us."[6] An image that carries such a connotation (and is therefore a symbol) is retained in our consciousness in vivid detail; when we recall it, we are visited with the emotion originally attendant with the image. The logo of the Red Cross or the Olympic games conveys a *feeling* derived from our experience. For most these would be mercy or international good will.

Good brands are of course symbols, but there are universal symbols that affect the psyche even more profoundly. This is why all religions employ symbolic language or images. A cross, a chalice, a Buddha, the star and crescent—all mean much more than their objective appearance.

James Joyce used this distinction in describing what he called "proper art" and "improper art." Improper art is common and in some way moves us to act. Modern advertising would fall into this category. Proper art, conversely, requires us to stand still, to enter into the feeling of what is behind the rendition.[7] In contrast, words and concepts are retained as mere ideas, unless they can hook our emotional involvement. Thus emotional commitment is unlikely to come from pie charts or data on PowerPoint slides. These electronic products are wonderful for display—and for allaying the fear of exposure and personal vulnerability—but they separate potential leaders from others and discourage real contact. The images we most vividly recall are not those from clip art or from the reflection of complex material on a screen. Rather, the images we remember are those we can see in a greater context of life, those created by human communication.

What we see and feel in one dimension can be translated to others through our imagination . . . our "ability to image." William Blake's words, "to see a universe in a grain of sand and eternity in an hour," accurately describe the symbolic perspective of the effective leader. Thoughtful leadership communication includes memorable images—images that at least approach the power of symbol, and sometimes actually attain it. For example, if you want to convey your company's desire to minimize the level of pesticides in oranges throughout the world, do you show the words "Minimize Pesticides in Oranges," show a picture of the machine that makes pesticides possible to detect, or show a young healthy child biting into an orange? The answer should be obvious. Some object to this idea as blatant false advertising, but it can be authentic—and when it is, it can be a powerful motivator.

A dramatic example reached the news in March 2012, when a federal judge in Washington delivered a judgment in a suit brought by several tobacco companies. The suit had sought a reversal of a federal mandate that the companies affix graphic photographic images to cigarette packaging. The nine color images depicted, among other things, a man exhaling cigarette smoke through a tracheotomy hole in his throat, a pair of diseased lungs next to a pair of healthy lungs; a diseased mouth afflicted with what appears to be cancerous lesions; and a cadaver on a table with post-autopsy chest staples. The tobacco companies were suing to stop the order based on the first amendment rights of free speech. Bear in mind that requiring stern printed warnings on packages was found to be constitutional in 1965. It was also true that none of the tobacco companies were claiming that the warnings of the printed material were incorrect—they admitted that cigarettes could cause cancer, birth defects, and other devastating illness, including the illnesses and conditions depicted in the images.

Judge Richard Leon ruled for the tobacco companies, drawing this distinction between the warning labels and the pictorial images. "The graphic images 'were neither designed to protect the consumer from confusion or deception, nor to increase consumer awareness of smoking risks; rather, *they were crafted to evoke a strong emotional response calculated to provoke the viewer to quit or never start smoking*'" (emphasis mine).[8] While the defense in this case argued that the judge got both the science and the law wrong, he clearly saw and articulated the difference in affect between a logical "fact-based" sentence and the emotional appeal of a provocative image.

I feel the need, from time to time, to affirm that I am not advocating an abandonment of words in favor of images; nor am I suggesting that facts and figures are not necessary. Indeed, they are. However, if we want to engage others emotionally as well as logically, we can heed the power of image and symbol and use that power as a supplement to help us communicate the emotional possibility of progress.

Analogy and Metaphor

Metaphor literally means to "carry across." Analogy and metaphor move us from a known to an unknown, or from the subjective to the objective. Is the building of the information superhighway in the nineties like the building of the automotive highway system in the fifties? Is cutting corporate cost to avoid layoffs like cutting family costs to avoid having college students come home for lack of tuition money? Is creating a national health care system analogous to creating the social security system? These analogies could be useful, as they point to both similarities and dissimilarities in a known and unknown situation, allowing people to learn by past experience rather than mere explanation.

Metaphor is to analogy as symbol is to image. Like symbol, metaphor offers something beyond the literal. Metaphor leaves out the "like" and just declares a truth that gets below the objective surface. It is the stuff of poetry—it encourages an experience that is greater than a mere surface comparison. Is love a flower, a bird, or a pothole? It is literally none of these, yet to express any of these as a truth is to convey an experience that will surely not be lost on listeners. They will learn the essence of love—love is beautiful, it blossoms, it is delicate, it soars on its own, challenges gravity, sings a beautiful song each day; love can be treacherous, can stop you in your tracks, can injure you. All these feelings can be experienced in the metaphors. Analogy and metaphor both bring a realization of the unknown from a reminder of the known, but the metaphor also provides an emotional understanding of the nature of a subjective feeling. The analogy states that competing in a marketplace is like conducting a war. The metaphor states that competition *is* war. Analogy invites comparison. Metaphor invites engagement.

Metaphor has four primary applications in leadership communication. One is the identification of the vision of the organization or movement you are trying to lead. In 1996, when Gil Amelio became CEO of Apple, he stated his metaphorical vision: Apple would become "the Maglite of the Computer Industry." Maglite made quality flashlights, and had indeed been given many industrial design awards, but Amelio needed to communicate his image to several thousand Apple employees, and it needed to be an image of a company with big margins, great reliability, and attractive designs. Few people at Apple knew anything about Maglite and the metaphor fell flat. Scott McNeely, long-term CEO of Sun Microsystems, drove his company to success and eventually down a steep grade with "Eat lunch or Be lunch." He also emphasized the "war" with Microsoft, a tough metaphor to come to work with every day. Mission metaphors can define your organization and determine whom you attract.[9]

In 2000, Karen Chang, then head of branches and business development for Charles Schwab, was addressing five hundred of her charges regarding their need to provide more specific customer solutions. Karen is one of the most respected women in American business—and in my view is also among the best-dressed. She used the following to make her point that her organization had to be more flexible to individual client needs: "We need to be more like Nordstrom. One customer can walk in needing an Armani suit, another might want some Donna Karan evening wear, and still another might simply want a Nordstrom's brand T-shirt. They can all be served in the same store." Karen's analogy got the point across in a succinct way, and a way that a major portion of her audience understood instantly. For those who might not, she continued: "Now I know that some of you guys didn't understand what I just said. You probably think that you saw 'Armani' on the menu at last night's Italian restaurant, and you've never heard of this 'Donna Karan' chick, but I'm tired of sports metaphors!" Very effective; extremely memorable.

A second application is to define a strategy or a tactic to focus others on what roles they play and what energy is needed. Depending on your choice of comparison, your communication can have very different results. Consider this choice. Suppose that you want to convey that your organization needs to become more proactive and less reactive. Which metaphor would resonate?

> "We need to get out of the foxholes and get up there and take that hill!"

> "We need to stop defending our own goal and get out there and score some of our own!"

"We need to stop wandering around the museum looking at paintings and get out there and create some masterpieces of our own!"

Each of these metaphors has an appeal, but the central point is that *people in the organization will identify with the metaphor you use.* If you use a military metaphor, then the enterprise is war, you are the general, they are the "grunts," and the stakes are life and death. This might not be the most productive atmosphere to be a part of for the long haul. Conversely, there are times in the cycle of most organizations when such a metaphor might well be appropriate.

If you use the sports metaphor then you are involved in a competitive game. You are the coach, they are the players, and the stakes are win or lose. This is why sports metaphors work so well—most people would rather play a competitive game and take the chance on losing than go to war with the risk of losing their lives.

The third example is for the creative professions. This enterprise is in creating and observing elegance in creativity. As the leader, you are either the master artist or a curator, each member of your team is a creative artist, and the enterprise is elegant innovation. It is not hard to see the metaphor's application in software development or research.

Choose analogy and metaphor carefully. Since people identify with these figures of speech immediately, and since these experiential referents have their roots of understanding in the limbic system, misstatements frequently result in misunderstandings—and at worst, they can create an understanding opposite from the truth.

In 2012, Mitt Romney referred to strategic focus in the primary as different from that of the general election. Eric Fehrnstrom, Romney's adviser, referred to the impending shift in strategy as an "Etch A Sketch" phenomenon. One had to question his understanding of the power of metaphor. Not only did the metaphor suggest constant flip-flop (complete with erasure), but by using a toy as a referent Fehrnstrom was also inviting even more assertions that Romney was condescending. To the detriment of his campaign the remark was referred to through both the primary and general elections.

A third, and perhaps the most important use for metaphor is to describe a compelling future. Again, choose with care, for some of the conclusions of those hearing you might be counterproductive for your cause. For example, when bioengineered food was initially becoming a possibility, food biotechnology experts were fond of drawing analogies between the development of genetically engineered food and the development of the monoclonal antibodies used in modern medicine. While the process is similar, few people want to consider food and medicine as equivalent. One executive even commented, "Within the next few years, you will be able to open your refrigerator and your medicine cabinet and see the same thing." This image was not helpful to his cause.

In fact, used intentionally, negative analogy or metaphor can bring home a real concern. Organized crime, budget deficits, and runaway costs are often referred to as "infectious diseases" or "cancers." These are both powerful metaphors, used frequently to emphasize progressive decay and potential death. Change is often referred to as "the tide" or "the wind," indicating a force that is beyond the listeners' control, but within their power to use for their own purpose. People fill in the attributes of the metaphor and assign them to the subject of discussion without further elaboration. Metaphors of few words create concrete images and make the abstract take form in the real world. Themes such as "climbing mountains" or "crossing chasms" can be used for multiple images and multiple connections.

Richard Mahoney, former chairman and CEO of Monsanto, spoke about innovation to the Council on Foreign Relations with these images: "Our freedom to innovate is being starved by tax and investment policies that eat our seed corn . . . rather than save it for planting." This real-world comparison has substantially more impact than the abstract translation of the facts: "Our freedom to innovate is being thwarted by policies that consume our investment capital."[10]

Finally, effective analogies can point others toward a conclusion that is in keeping with your intent. In 1992, NASA Administrator Daniel Goldin addressed the Association of Space Explorers in Washington, D.C., on the question of why the United States should send a human expedition to Mars. In setting the stage for his advocacy, he drew the following analogy from the time of Columbus's voyage:

> Only [Queen] Isabella was willing to look beyond the many problems on her own shores, and see the potential reward for her investment in the future. The voyages of Columbus set the stage for more Spanish explorers, who turned Spain into a great world power. As a consequence, the language and culture of Spain prevail in most of Latin America to this day.
>
> On the other side of the world, however, in China . . . the intended destination of Columbus . . . their emperors turned their backs on the rest of the world. Sixty years prior to 1492, Chinese explorers had traveled as far as Africa. But a new emperor considered such journeys wasteful extravagances. His successors burned the boats, and banned all Chinese from leaving the country. Those who tried could be executed.
>
> That 15th century decision to *not* explore still reverberates in China today. What was one of the world's most advanced and innovative civilizations is today an inward-looking nation. For a country with the most people on Earth, it is almost an afterthought in global affairs.[11]

Much has happened since Goldin's comments, and China could hardly be accused of having an inward focus today. Still, this is an apt historical comparison because the conclusions are unmistakable. The nation that has the foresight to explore space will lead progress in other areas as well. Going to Mars may not be the logically correct decision for the United States, but certainly at some point, someone *will* send human beings to another planet, and it is possible that other nations will then be forever catching up to the nations that demonstrated more courage and foresight.

Whether for a vision, for a strategy or tactic, or to describe a compelling future or warn of a disaster, a leader chooses analogies and metaphors knowing that the entire organization will be influenced by the choice. Whether these comparisons have resonance is largely a function of the experience of those who hear the analogies and metaphors, whether they are familiar with the shared characteristics, and whether they react positively or negatively to those characteristics. Metaphors are never just general;

they are personal in their appeal. Karen Chang did it well. Had Gil Amelio gone on to explain his reference to Maglite, perhaps even personally distributing some of these exquisite pieces to Apple employees, he might well have created an entire communication platform based on his observation. But he did not explain it, and it fell flat.

Narrative as Connection—Myth, Story, and Experience

Twentieth-century political theorist and philosopher Hannah Arendt observed, "Story-telling reveals meaning without committing the error of defining it."[12] Indeed, "Tell me a story" is the most repeated refrain in millions of households around the world every night. We want to hear tales of success, of heroes, of tragedy. Hardly anyone says, "Will you read me a few bedtime concepts?" Concepts don't create resonance; stories do. Leadership communication is about "growth" and "progress," words that contain a past, a present, and a future—a story line.

Despite the universal scientific evidence and our collective intuitive sense that time is an illusion, it is, as Einstein said, "a most *stubborn* illusion." The journey through space and time is basic in its import; it is part of the unseen atmosphere of our very existence without regard to culture. The story is to most humans like water is to fish: so integral to existence that only our self-reflective ability allows us to see it. Everyone's life lies between some version of "once upon a time," and "they all lived happily ever after." Because stories are about our lives, they inspire us with possibility. When leaders build them liberally into communication, others have the opportunity to identify with the story and all of its elements . . . and change it to make the story come true for them as well.

Myths: Creating Cultural Values

Myths are a most particular type of story, not literally true but metaphorically effective and broad-gauged. Myth is symbolic and steeped in meaning, so the nature of myth is more important as we define the nature of communication that connects with multiple cultures, and even more deeply as symbolic (creating meaning that is inherent in our existence).

Joseph Campbell defined the purpose of myth as fourfold. First, to reconcile our lives to what we actually see as the nature of life in the world. Early myths about the constellations moving through the heavens are examples of these myths . . . they helped the ancients make sense of their physical world, including birth and death. Myths about all of nature's phenomena accomplished the same function, and humans frequently personified these energies into Gods and Goddesses. We still have myths that help us reconcile our values with what is observable in life. Hence the creators of *Star Wars, Harry Potter, Lord of the Rings,* and other classics crafted personifications of good and evil, of the magical and the mundane, and of the hero and the heroine and the villain, in order to retell myths that have been with us since the dawn of consciousness.

The second function of myth that Campbell identifies is to present an image of the cosmos "that will maintain and elicit an experience of awe."[13] This is a mystical function that recognizes that which we have yet to explain—the mystery of life itself. We can only point to it, theorize about it, and tell a plausible story that is consistent with the state of our scientific understanding. There are few scientists, however, who believe we will ever be able to define, cognitively and without question, the origins or fate of our universe.

When my sons were young, we would frequently stretch out in a field across from our house and look at the stars, or during our annual fishing trips to Montana, take advantage of the "big sky" to imagine even more broadly. For them (and for me) it was hard to grasp that what we were seeing at that moment had actually happened millions or billions of years ago. The scale of the universe comes alive with this type of activity, just as it does with any story that sparks our sense of awe at the ultimate mystery. Myth is the story that we make up to explain this mystery.

The third function of myth, one that is central to my purpose here, is to "validate and maintain a certain sociological system: a shared set of rights and wrongs, proprieties or improprieties, on which your particular social unit depends for its existence."[14] These myths are, for example, about the nature of capitalism, whether humankind is a steward, a participant, or has dominion over nature. In the United States, myth is the basis for statements like "We hold these truths to be self-evident."

The fourth function of mythology is psychological. The myth must carry the individual through the stages of life, from birth through maturity through old age to death. The mythology must do so in accord with the social order, the cosmos as understood by the group, and what Campbell refers to as "the monstrous mystery that is existence."[15]

I went back to graduate school in 2004 to understand the universal nature of myths and archetypes in order to help leaders increase their scale of effectiveness. Most of these global stories operate below the surface of consciousness. Just as the Judeo-Christian myths operate below the consciousness of the West and in Islam, systems of religion and mythology in other parts of the world are literally "baked in" to the society. Biblical and Koran stories in the monotheistic traditions are mirrored with elaborate stories from the Mahabharata and Ramayana in Hindu civilization, "Monkey" from the oral traditions of narrative in the religions of Buddhism, Confucianism, and Shintoism, and in the myriad personified stories in the nature-based ancient religions of Africa, now also popular and practiced throughout the southern hemisphere. Some understanding of these fundamental stories is a requisite for global leadership. It is also a worthwhile study for anyone wishing to inspire others with varied backgrounds. Knowing these stories will help you understand what might be important topics for your own stories, the ones you will use in your Personal Leadership Communication Guide.

Story: Closer to the Everyday

Because they define civilizations, myths change very slowly, but our more mundane stories are more facile. We make up stories that reflect the way things are, and a leader's task is to move from the status quo to a place defined as progress. Because my education included an emphasis in depth psychology (the psychology of Jung, Adler, and more recently James Hillman), I occasionally attend programs for therapists on myth and story as methods of healing. In one such program, the director, Jonathan Young, suggested to the therapists that their patients were really looking for editors. "When they come to you," he said, "they are saying 'I don't like my story. Can you help me change it?'"

This is actually the task of the leader: to edit the story of the organization, to change the ending, to infuse a new plot line into a story that has become stale, lifeless, or irrelevant. It is not done by merely adding some people, firing some others, and rearranging the talent. As discussed in Chapter Seven, describing a new future is one application of story; others are inspiring new behavior, building a new culture, or preserving the past. Business literature is rich in urban legends, stories of great brands: how the FedEx employee hired a helicopter on his own, or the UPS driver found the artist and had a damaged painting repaired for a client in time for Christmas, or the most famous of all, the Nordstrom's employee who gave an elderly lady a credit for faulty tires that her former husband had purchased on the Nordstrom's site before the store was built. Stories will help others experience the need for change and the excitement of being part of it. Your Guide has to include stories to ground whatever other evidence you might offer.

Personal Stories About Others—Convincing Evidence

Stories that illustrate the change that is needed, the reason for change, or the effect of change will resonate deeply with others. In fact, stories have been shown to be a most powerful form of evidence. A study conducted by organizational psychologists Joanne Martin and Melanie Powers concluded that a story provided more credibility to a proposition than a mere declaration by an executive, data alone, or data combined with the same story. In their study, they asserted to four distinct groups of people that a particular company had followed a practice of no layoffs for its entire history. To prove this proposition, they offered one group the data, and to another a simple statement by a senior executive. A third group simply heard a story of a long-term employee, and the fourth got all of the data and heard the story as well. The group that heard only the story were the most convinced.[16] Why would this be the case?

Given modern knowledge of the brain, it seems reasonable to conclude that the limbic system is the receptor of analog data, like stories, while digital data needs to be processed by the cortex. When presented with digital data, the cortex does what it is supposed to do . . . analyze, doubt, and judge as ways of reaching the correct decision. Conversely, analog data like the story does not require judgment or decision. Imagine telling a story around the campfire and hearing someone say, “Oh, I disagree with that!” It doesn’t make sense.

Here’s an example. I feel very strongly about the value of community, and whenever I am speaking with people about it, advocating a less mobile and hectic way of life, I tell this story of my former father-in-law:

> Harry Magner was orphaned in the 1920s, when he and his brother were in their early teens. At the time they were living in Seattle, but they had an aunt and uncle in Buffalo. They had a used Model T Ford, and drove the car east from Washington to New York, working when they needed cash to buy food and gasoline. It took them over a month to make the journey.
>
> When they arrived in Buffalo, the boys enrolled in high school. The next year, Harry met Marge. They were married just out of school; Harry went to work for the local bank, and they were able to buy a house in the suburbs. Harry and Marge had a son, and then twin daughters. They joined the local church where Harry served as treasurer, youth group leader, and deacon.
>
> They never moved their home. For the next sixty years, they lived in the same house, raised three well-adjusted children, traveled a little with friends, played cards often, and served in just about every capacity that the community offered. Harry retired from the bank after more than forty years on the job. He died of cancer at home when he was eighty. He was cheerful to the end, and his house was full of friends and family when his spirit left the earth.
>
> While Harry was alive, he was the happiest and most grateful person I knew. Several hundred people attended his funeral. He rarely left Buffalo; he didn’t accomplish anything that will be printed in a history book; yet the accolades about his love

and devotion to family and community set a benchmark for my own life. His oldest friend present at the funeral had known him for more than seventy years.

Plenty of data record the delinquency rates of kids who move a lot. Plenty of surveys track the happiness of people who stay in communities for long periods of time. If I were advocating a change in policy that would allow people to remain in their communities, this data would be valuable, but it would not replace the story of Harry Magner. I'm sure that as you read this story, you were relating to it in some way. If you have moved a lot, you might have been reflecting on the consequences. You might have been thinking of parents or friends who have also had the experience of living in one place for a long time. Certainly, you weren't trying to figure out if my numbers were accurate, or wondering about the source of my information.

To most of us, stories are reality; certainly much more so than some concepts, data, or a few insights. Using stories to communicate links us with others on a human plane.

Connecting Through Personal Experience

While we can relate to others effectively with stories about situations regarding other people in our lives, connection will be strongest when what we have to say is real—when we can relate our own relevant personal experience. Metaphor is twice removed, like a copy of a photographic print. Story is once removed, like the negative itself. The personal experience of someone we are directly communicating with is the real thing, not removed at all; and because leadership is personal, the leader's life experience is, without doubt, the best grist for authentic connection.

I can illustrate from my own experience.

One of my own fundamental values is the freedom and ability to express oneself fully. I'm passionate about this subject, probably as a result of being the smallest kid in my school classes, feeling like I had to speak louder than other kids to be heard. I was also raised on a farm, where each member of the family subordinated his will for the good of the family enterprise. As a final influence, I had an older brother who was substantially larger than I was, and who was occasionally willing to use his size to make sure his little brother didn't become a pest. We had always been close, but his early influence contributed to my later need to be heard. In short, it seemed that few circumstances of my early life encouraged me to speak. Therein lies the source of my passion for self-expression. Accordingly, throughout my corporate and teaching career, I've been a proponent of building skills for developing other people, or, in today's jargon, "empowerment."

As a result of this passion for self-expression, I have done some analysis of the components of good delegation. While most authorities on this subject correctly identify the objective components of teaching, giving authority, and assigning responsibility, few have acknowledged the subjective or emotional components of delegation. Clearly, when real delegation occurs, the boss feels a sense of insecurity, some anxiety that the job will not get done properly. The boss also might feel some loss, as the delegation means letting the student go, no longer connected by the tether of the teaching relationship.

I advocate the use of subjective measurements to confirm that the boss has truly empowered someone else. I maintain that if you have taught someone well and then given them complete authority and responsibility, you will feel some anxiety and loss. I can offer data in support of this assertion, but the most compelling evidence is my own profound experience of delegating as a parent. Since everyone in my audience has been a child, and many of them are currently parents, they inevitably relate to this narrative:

> In 1982, I became a single parent, and had sole custody and responsibility for my two sons, then thirteen and eleven years old. For the next few years, we grew uncommonly close through a series of personal trials. I had left my career at IBM and finances were particularly tight; then I had remarried too hurriedly and caused some further anxiety. Nonetheless, the boys had done well in school and in life, having formed fast friendships and developed solid values. I took tremendous pride (and still do) in their attitude toward life and in the way they conduct themselves.
>
> My oldest son, Jeff, was admitted to the University of California at San Diego in the fall of 1986, and I elected to drive him to school from San Francisco, a distance of

approximately five hundred miles. It was September, but still hot in California's central valley along Interstate 5. We drove the ten hours, making small talk and generally cracking nervous jokes. I tried to be serious about the future a couple of times, but found Jeff only interested in the next months of testing his ability to fend for himself, a very natural concern.

We arrived at the campus in midafternoon and I helped him move into his dorm room, the oldest housing on campus but in a choice location and setting. It faced a large square carpet of grass in a quadrangle perimetered by six two-story green buildings. On this particular day, it was sparkling with the nervous laughter of new students and the brilliant colors of Southern California clothes.

I helped him move his stuff into a second-story room and started playing "Mr. Mom." I hung pictures, made his bed, and unpacked his Eagle Scout mug. In my concentration I had failed to notice the growing contingent of kids in the hall, the escalating sound of music, and the lack of interest on his part in what I was doing. To Jeff's credit, he was very patient, but when his roommate arrived and they began to compare histories, I realized that I had overstayed. We agreed that I would come back that evening to take him to dinner, and I returned to the hotel for a swim. I was beginning to feel anxious.

That evening, just at sunset, I made my way back across the quad to his room. As I approached, I could see the lights of his room and hear the music of the growing gathering of excited newcomers. By now the group was co-ed and there was some dancing in the common area. It was difficult to get his attention as I stood in his room door.

Of course, everything I had done was changed. The beds were on opposite sides of the room, the pictures had been replaced with posters, and the Eagle Scout mug was not to be seen. He was engaged in conversation with a group of three students and clearly not pining away for an early dinner with his Dad.

I finally waved an arm and he joined me in the hall. I suggested that rather than go to dinner he should stay with his friends and that I would see him in the morning for breakfast before I had to return up the coast. He protested just enough, then agreed, letting me know that he was looking forward to breakfast.

I left, and hurried down the stairs and into a nearby grove of eucalyptus trees, where I walked alone and cried for about an hour and a half.

This was true delegation. I had done my best to train this young man for the task ahead. I now had to give up any aspect of control over his life and let him live it. My role would be only to respond, not to direct. And because I loved him, it hurt.

I've relayed this experience many times. It never fails to connect me to my own conviction on the subject, and it never fails to connect me with others. Everyone can see themselves in one of the roles in the experience. The feelings that these events engender not only strengthen my advocacy, they also provide a convincing realization that true delegation is difficult; that in the absence of a certain amount of rich and wonderful emotional pain, delegation probably doesn't happen. Because I had this experience and am able to connect it metaphorically with other instances of delegation, I can speak on this subject with a great deal of intensity.

Taking Jeff to college was only one experience. My parents' values, my upbringing, my parents' deaths, my experience on the farm, my successes and failures as an athlete and scholar, my choice of college, my studies, playing music, my children's births, my career at IBM, running across the United States, trips to the old Soviet Union, the times when I have been hurt, elated, sick, married, divorced . . . these and *all* of the other less notable experiences of my life have formed the convictions that compel me to speak. Fortunately, my biography is not yet over. Experiences that I have today will help form the basis for my conviction in years to come.

So it is with you. Using the relevant experiences of your life to support your advocacy for change is the most effective way of connecting to your own conviction and assuring an authentic bond with others. All this belongs in your Leadership Communication Guide.

The Rules of Engagement—Authenticity Is Paramount

As powerful as stories and experiences are, they are fraught with potential for manipulation. This is all the more reason to be careful as you develop any change message. Stories can be made up and then generalized illegitimately in an attempt to prove a point. Without data, such generalization is only manipulation. Relating personal experience can also be manipulative and even substantially detract from a leader's credibility. Remember that we now know that our brains actually can and do recognize intention—although we are not always conscious of that fact. Everyone has had that feeling, when they are communicating, that something is off, there is a lack of understanding, something unsaid, but few of us have the courage to say so in the moment. To others to whom a leader relates, nothing is so clearly inauthentic as an attempt to move them with a disingenuous story or experience. Here are some guidelines to help avoid these pitfalls.

The experience must be clearly relevant to the point you are making. My former colleague Harvey Stone likes to refer to the sharing of irrelevant stories as "therapy"—and it certainly can have that flavor. If the experience you relate does not support your advocacy, others lose interest.

Personal experiences must be related from memory, not from a script. When I begin the story of taking Jeff to college, I transport myself through imagination back to the car, back to the central valley of California. With my son in the passenger's seat, I relate what I see and feel during that reverie. I know that the images in my memory will generate a legitimate emotional response in me, and I know that others will respond in a much more holistic way to that actual memory than to a recitation. Consider, would someone you trust read you a report of a real incident, or tell you of experiencing that incident?

When his son was injured in a tragic accident in the late 1980s, soon-to-be vice president Al Gore was often interviewed about the impact of the incident on his life and his political career. His answers were always spontaneous, authentic, and touching. Clearly this incident was a turning point in Gore's maturity as a human being. Unfortunately, the version that he told at the 1992 Democratic Convention was cued and rehearsed, and to anyone who had heard the story authentically, its staging there felt like a mere emotional appeal for support. There was a calculated personal tone, aimed at manipulating rather than connecting, and to me, it hurt Gore's human credentials. Had he simply left the script and read from his internal memory of the day of the accident, letting the camera operators fend for themselves to find Gore's son in the candidate's box, he might well have connected with himself again, and therefore with the audience as well. Regardless of how compelling the facts of a story are, the reporting of those facts and the emotional authenticity will trump the circumstances themselves.

When the Republican candidates were debating in the 2012 primary, one seemed strident and aloof, one seemed like an unyielding zealot, while another, the favorite, couldn't seem to connect with any consistency. He presented himself as defended and proper, and I for one wished I could see the real person just once. I realize that press coverage, innuendo, and a constant stream of news might make such an approach frightening. Still, I longed for a connection, as I believe others did.

Another rule of engagement is to leave nothing out. The memory of a substantive experience includes all aspects of the original happening, the sensory-rich details that guide the imagination of those you are relating to and bring your own passion to the surface. Exactly what you saw and heard, exactly what you perceived and felt; these minutiae will turn the experience into one that taps your own heart and the collective heart of others.

Finally, when relating personal experience, you have to use the first person. Revert to "you," "they," or "one" and your message becomes an opinion rather than a reality, an example rather than an experience. Others might get the lesson, but they will miss the connection that is so vital to hearing your authentic voice.

***

Connecting with others—creating limbic resonance—is largely dependent on your choice to be vulnerable and authentic in what you communicate. The content of the message will determine what comes of that connection. The next chapters provide a framework for content, specific instructions for asking yourself the right questions to assure that your Communication Guide is complete, and some examples that will give you the experience to make your leadership communication both clear and deep.

Chapter Four

Writing—Applying Discipline to Authenticity

So far, I've defined the essence of leadership as making an emotional connection with others to build commitment toward creating a new imagined future. In emphasizing the need for leaders to display both competence and connection, the focus has been on ways to create emotional resonance. The reason for the emphasis is twofold. First, people might be convinced through their conceptual capability, but they commit from their emotions. By connecting with others we tap this emotional energy. In *How We Decide,* Jonah Lehrer boils it down like this: "The emotional brain is especially useful at helping us make hard decisions. Its massive computational power—its ability to process millions of bits of data in parallel—ensures that you can analyze all the relevant information when assessing alternatives."[1]

Equally important is to engage ourselves emotionally; as we do, we stimulate and strengthen our own resolve, creating a deep well of passion to drink from during the process of rolling out a plan. Positive emotion will reinforce our own commitment and make the change we are advocating more than just a good idea. Instructions for carrying out that plan are important, but feeling the *why* of it, the meaning of such a change, will provide the power to get it done. Central to crossing this resonance boundary with others is your own authenticity.

Writing as a Process

The best way to discover authenticity and express relevance about a change that you want to implement is to write. In writing, we simultaneously discover what we want to say.

The chapters of Part Two explore the components of a Personal Leadership Communication Guide, a document that will include all the material that is relevant and necessary for you to communicate with others about your proposed change. This document is not a speech, a memo, an essay, or an article, but all of these could come from the material you create for it. The Guide is a dynamic and never-finished piece of writing that serves as your own source of information and impressions that will inspire you and others around a particular change. It includes your own inner convictions, your strongest evidence, all the elements that would be relevant to the issue itself, your passion about it, and the foundation of your connection to others.

This type of writing is not a normal habit of the Western leader, particularly in business, nor is it practiced frequently in any other culture. In general, we find ourselves communicating in the jargon and cultural norm of some organization, rather than from our inner, natural language.

Still, when we rediscover the magic of revelatory self-expression, we feel right at home with it. Without exception, everyone who has engaged in this work has found it valuable both personally and professionally.

Early in 1998, I was introduced to Ed Jensen, soon to be retired as president and CEO of Visa International. Ed was completing a sterling career in financial services and was planning to move and reshape his work life into more humanitarian endeavors, focused around creating economic renewal in less-than-affluent neighborhoods.

We met for drinks at the Huntington Hotel in San Francisco to discuss his plans for retirement and explore ways we might work together. He was interested in the whole idea of authentic leadership, given that volunteers are much more challenging to lead than are people who depend on you for a paycheck. Volunteers work for meaning, not for money. The question of how to inspire that kind of loyalty was an important one for Ed and he had great instincts about it.

We spoke about authentic communication, and after some discussion of the difficulty of applying it in a business context, we agreed that one of the best sources of this kind of communication is poetry. With few exceptions, poets write because they have something to say, not because there is a market for it, and because of that motivation, their writing generally touches us in ways that other writing does not. We read poetry just as we listen to birds sing, with anticipation of the next note, not with judgment about how good others will find it. Many of the best poets will also admit that they write to discover themselves. Often the last line is not obvious when a poet begins a work.

Ed said that he had written some poetry in secondary school and college, but that he had not written that way in years. He then told me a story.

His father had died a few months before our meeting, and Ed had to sort through the attic at the family house. He had come across a folder with letters in it, and began to read the first one casually. He saw that it was an essay . . . a letter of acknowledgment to his parents for their sacrifice and love. He was into the second page before he realized that he was the author; he had written it as part of some final assignments in college.

"I could never write that essay today," he said. "Everything I write now sounds like a memo."

My mind went to my own bookshelves and writings, as I reflected on the number of times I had expressed this same frustration in my own longing and search for authenticity. After our conversation, I sent Ed a poem of Derek Walcott's, reprinted here with permission.

Love After Love

The day will come
when, with elation,
you will greet yourself arriving
at your own door, in your own mirror,
and each will smile at the other's welcome,

and say, sit here. Eat.

You will love again the stranger who was your self.
Give wine. Give bread. Give back your heart
to itself, to the stranger who has loved you

all your life, whom you ignored
for another, who knows you by heart.
Take down the love letters from the bookshelf,

the photographs, the desperate notes,
peel your image from the mirror.
Sit. Feast on your life.[2]

Ed sent me a return e-mail: "Thank you for sending the poem about me." His comment inspired me to read, write, and examine more poets to uncover their particular gift and determine how it could help those who would be leaders.

As Ed had hinted, at some time in our lives, usually at a relatively young age, those of us who are *not* poets lose our real voice and adopt a more conventional one in the legitimate desire to communicate in some new context. Unfortunately, that altered voice can take over completely—suddenly twenty years have gone by and we have missed many opportunities to use our real voice, the one that belongs to the stranger "who has loved you all of your life," the stranger Walcott and the rest of us see in the mirror.

I spoke to Ed again in February 2012. He is thriving and has done some wonderful work in the last few years, serving on several financially related boards as well as that of Lewis and Clark College in Portland, Oregon. Ed seemed equally excited about serving on panels at a Leadership Academy in Cabo San Lucas, Mexico. Started by Jerry Nelson, a former developer in Arizona and a co-founder of TicketMaster, the academy brings together a hundred students at a time for a week of exposure to leadership practices. Panelists at the academy include some of the world's most renowned leaders, including Ed.

Ed's early observation about his own change in self-expression was a great gift to me, and as we spoke this time, both of us nearly fifteen years older than when we first met, we wondered aloud whether we still can access the inspiration to start new things and change ourselves. His musing brought to mind yet another poem, this one by Stanley Kunitz, written when he was in his nineties. In "The Layers" Kunitz is asking essentially the same question that Ed asked: "Can we continue to bloom new blooms?" Kunitz answers himself after comparing all the efforts that he has made, the poems he has offered, to steps in a long journey. As he pauses to look back, he is amazed at the length of the journey he has made, and is clear about his next move: "Yet I turn, I turn,/exulting somewhat,/with my will intact to go/wherever I need to go,/ and every stone on the road/precious to me.[3]

Like Kunitz's, Ed's words made it obvious that he is still at it—still being inspired and passing inspiration along to others.

Your Voice Comes Through

Sooner or later, if we are lucky, that person we once were comes forward again, sometimes without waiting for permission. Fortunately, that neglected voice has real power, and will generally come out whether we like it or not.

As a young man in my thirties, I was running a fairly large sales operation for IBM on the West Coast of the United States. My fifteen-year career with the company had been studded with success, but I had made a lifestyle decision to move back to the West Coast in the mid-1970s, and didn't intend to move east again. Accordingly, my interest in my job had been waning. I was ready to leave, and I was being helped along by the growing bureaucracy of the firm.

At that time, all companies doing interstate commerce were required by the federal government to compile extensive reports on the status of their Equal Opportunity efforts. Unfortunately, this onerous reporting requirement had soured most managers, and the bureaucratic process had received far more attention than the real work of hiring and promoting minorities. In January of that year, a well-meaning HR vice president had instituted yet one more layer of reporting, requiring all managers to have written development plans on file for each person in their organization who was in an "affected class," essentially women and minorities. This requirement became an exercise in filling out forms rather than stimulating any real extra effort at authentic career counseling and development. Those managers already doing the job of developing their people now merely had an extra burden.

Each quarter, the nine of us responsible for our division's national results reviewed our progress with senior management in New Jersey. At the third-quarter review that year, the vice president who had instituted the development plan requirement entered the meeting and asked us what we thought of it. He was obviously looking for agreement. I heard a voice say, "I think it is the biggest bunch of B.S. I've ever seen." It was a full five seconds before I realized that it had been my voice uttering these words. Clearly my career was in serious jeopardy, and in the following mini-seconds that seemed like hours, I knew that I didn't care.

The next voice, after a stunned silence, was that of my boss and mentor, Ed Mosner. "I couldn't agree with you more," he said. "How would you like to fix it?"

Most people have experienced some moment similar to this, either vicariously or personally. Finding one's voice is not the same as discovering values, but often in that moment of frustration when values are violated, the voice can't be stopped. Popeye, the sailor cartoon character of old, was known for such moments of frustration. He was patient to a point, but when pushed to the wall by his cartoon rival, or when his friend and love Olive Oyl was threatened, he would raise his right index finger high, puff his cheeks, and mutter, "That's all I can stands, I can't stands no more!" Out would come a can of spinach, he would down it in one swallow, and proceed to take care of the situation, usually with physical force.

Such moments of expression are mythical, in that they signal a "coming of age," a willingness to "stand" for something. In literature, theater, art, and motion pictures, these moments are depicted to inspire us, as people throw their lives, or in my case, their careers, into the flame of conviction about an issue. Whether it is Todd Anderson (in the movie *Dead Poets Society*) standing on his desk to defend his teacher, Mr. Keating, an impassioned William Wallace sounding a battle cry for Scotland, or Harry Potter, the boy who survived the attack of evil and eventually defeated it, magically, with his internal powers—the meaning is clear: some things are worth speaking out for, worth metaphorically dying for. And money, prestige, and safety cannot stand in their way.

Because Ed Mosner valued authenticity over politics, his response to my outburst was positive. I might not have been so fortunate. Many are not. Yet people who take stands based upon their beliefs have moved closer to leadership. They are clear about what matters, and they have mustered the courage to speak in defense of that value.

But being impetuous is not leading. I could hardly claim that my outburst about the development plan inspired anyone. Horrified, yes. Inspired, no. Ed's act of grace extended my career by two years, and I did indeed get involved in emphasizing the "doing" part of development over the "reporting" part of development. As I began the task of turning the bureaucratic process into some meaningful result, I realized I had to communicate about it in a different way. Ranting and raving about bureaucracy wasn't going to work. Many people were emotionally invested in the process in place, and most were skeptical about making any change at all. I would need a disciplined and inclusive approach to get anyone's attention, and my communication would have to reflect something far greater than merely changing a reporting procedure if I were to inspire others to act. I had to not only show competence but also stay connected to what was meaningful and communicate from that principle.

It wasn't hard to discover that the value that had been violated by this suggested practice was authenticity. In this case, the leaders of my division of IBM had been unconsciously promoting form over substance, letting convention get in the way of actually making a difference. We had been going through the motions. To lead our way out, my basic message had to be supported by the flaw in that motivation and my commitment to change it. The message had to be clear and deep, and I had to craft it well before I could begin to deliver it.

My Leadership Communication Guide included not only the facts and history of job discrimination, but also my writing about the strength of my own feeling about authenticity, and about the value of providing equal opportunity as a fundamental right of being an American. My trips to the Jefferson Memorial started to have real meaning in a context other than my own life. These values had the power to connect me with others, pulling them into the issue on the basis of values—not dwelling on whether the current system was the best, only focusing on what could change to make it better.

While the requirement for the development plans stayed in place, the spirit of completing them changed, and the enforcement of the practice took on a completely different tone. A few years later, the federal government dropped the requirement for the extensive reporting. Although I had left IBM long before, I was sure that the managers who were involved in this change were still doing the right thing for the right reason. They were not just filling out forms.

Only by disciplining your voice can you allow real leadership to emerge. It isn't necessary to wait for your voice to assert itself without your help. In fact, as I can attest, it's better not to wait for that Popeye moment. It is far better to decide what your values compel you to change and then start writing.

Documenting Competence and Connection

The insights gleaned through reflection demand the discipline of writing before they can be converted into action. While off-the-cuff conversations can be authentic, they often relay only a momentary emotional impulse. For example, we have all heard public speakers who can "light a fire" in an audience. When these speakers are finished, everyone in the room wants to do *something*, but no one knows what to do. This same eruptive kind of communication takes place in informal meetings in offices around the world and many of us scramble to comply. Practitioners garner nicknames that portray their style—"Old Ironsides," or "Neutron Jack."

Communication that moves others to committed action includes both passion and reason. Both are necessary to generate trust and action from others, so that the mind is as fully engaged as the heart. Writing is imperative to this process. It reveals fuzzy thinking, exposes slurred distinctions: it clarifies, and it can move us to both greater clarity and greater passion. As you work on writing the Guide you can actually experience resistance that might arise. That's why preparing the Guide can be difficult and why it takes time, more time to write than to make a few notes.

In 2012, Matt Hyde was an executive at REI known for his ability to inspire. He and his wife, both mountain climbers, spend many hours in a small tent waiting for sunrise or for a storm to clear. "It's a good thing," says Matt, "because I spend a lot of time thinking, and then writing what I am thinking and feeling about any major change." When I spoke with him, Matt was leading a complete revision of the REI Outlet online store, a presence he first created in 1993. In place for fifteen years, the site was well known to the staff and customers alike, so this alteration will be seen and experienced as a major change. The week after we spoke, he was also to address eighty-five graduates of the Harvard Business School on the difference between a straight for-profit business and a co-op, and the following week he was to give a one-hour presentation to a leadership conference in Seattle. Each of these presentations represented the same values—customer loyalty, the values and vision of REI, and the advantages of the co-op form of doing business, but each required a distinctly different approach. Matt places such a high value on communication that it takes him an *hour to write and prepare for each minute of a presentation.* He understands that the renditions from this kind of investment of time and thought yield much deeper and effective communication.

In between these more formal occasions, Matt was communicating spontaneously with employees, customers, the press, and multiple other constituents. He depended on his faithful and informal documentation to anticipate and respond in these less formal and more extemporaneous situations.

Matt's discipline includes regular journaling to document stories, a process encouraged by his leadership coach Sherryl Christie-Bierschenk. This was a hard habit to develop, but now Matt realizes that he rarely knows when a particular story or piece of data will be a useful inspirational tool. These informal musings feed his formally prepared and written presentations. For example, in preparing to introduce Richard Louv, a well-known writer on the value of open space and outdoor experiences for kids with attention deficit disorder, to a group of REI customers and employees, Matt referred to his own journal.[4] A few weeks earlier he had been with the head of the Municipal Park System in Detroit. Because of the dedication of this one man, Detroit has one of the best park systems in the United States. In fact, the largest Detroit municipal park is five times bigger than Discovery Park, the largest park in Seattle—not a fact most would guess, given the industrial reputation of Detroit and the green culture of Seattle. In his introduction of the author, Matt used the story of that meeting to emphasize how one person could vastly improve the outdoor experience for all, even in a metropolis like Detroit. Writing, recording impressions, remarking on incidents, articulating values—all grist for the mill of inspiration—all belong in the Guide.

Reflection, writing, and including the elements of a framework only provide the vehicle for real self-expression. Following the instructions does not guarantee authenticity, it only makes it possible. The discipline presented here is like musical notation. It has form, and it can evoke beauty, but the real meaning of any musical performance can only be brought forth by the musician.

In the early 1990s, Robert Commanday, then music critic for the *San Francisco Chronicle,* illustrated this principle in a critique of a young Russian violinist, Vadim Repin, who had played Tchaikovsky's Violin Concerto in D Major with the San Francisco Symphony Orchestra. I had been in the audience, and as a former violinist, I found Repin's technique flawless. He was fast and precise, and drew a standing ovation. But I had noticed only a few phrases of the music when the distinction between the instrument, the violinist, the orchestra, and the music disappeared. As it turned out, those moments were also noticed by the critic and used as a contrast with the rest of the performance.

Commanday's critique read, in part, as follows (emphasis mine):

> Repin has a grand, exceptionally big, warm tone, a phenomenal technique that commanded this concerto, even challenging the finale to go as vivacissimo as the orchestra can play it. *Hiding somewhere underneath that there must be a personality, a musician with something to say of his own.* . . . He played most of the first movement cadenza as if smoothness in

> bowing . . . were the principal expressive idea. [But] after the cadenza, Repin began to set off and reveal the phrases.
>
> The Finale was a rouser, faster and faster, keener and keener, and the audience loved it. [But] the musicality must develop alongside the technique and purely violinistic mastery and be there the whole way . . . yes . . . at 21, the essential matter is not just how he plays but why.[5]

A master violinist's reading and playing of a musical score does not ensure his self-expression through the instrument. Your writing a Personal Leadership Communication Guide in full does not ensure the emergence of your authentic voice, but it will prompt, cajole, and at some point assist you to know where the facts and feelings come together to have maximum impact.

Musical notation and words only represent the real thing. After you have written your convictions, you must communicate them from the inside out, bringing your own internal voice to the symbols on the page.

Authentic communication is a continual dance between the heart and the mind, and between you and those with whom you communicate. Your own engagement in the subject will provide a mirror of what you are engendering in others. As you are passionate, convinced, and committed about the change you want to make, so others can become passionate, convinced, and committed as they engage with you around your message.

***

Before you go public, your message needs your life *and* your ideas. The words you use and the way you relate them will determine whether you will be perceived as a leader or merely as a person with a lot of passion around a good idea, whether you want to inspire others or merely get results. The demands of the process will make your passion clear and your message concise. Part Two explores the mechanics and guides you through the process.

Part Two

The Personal Leadership Communication Guide: Biography with a Purpose

The chapters of Part Two provide practical instruction on preparing a comprehensive guide for inspiring communication. To benefit fully, select a specific change that you want to implement, and then follow the instructions given in the next chapters. Because this Guide calls for elements of both competence and trustworthiness, it is biographical as well as situational. The process of preparing it asks you to relate your values to the change you are proposing even as you are constructing the logical case. Thus you will need to find, prepare, and document material that will be the grist for communication in every venue.

These chapters ask for and demonstrate the use of symbol and image, metaphor and analogy, and story, personal experience, and myth, and they show how these elements relate to the data and circumstances of the situation. All of them work together to build trust in you and to inspire others to engage in the change you are leading. The Guide becomes the foundation for all of your leadership communication as you go forward.

Consider these chapters as a "questioning machine" for your use. If you have carefully considered the questions, and if you have answered these questions authentically in writing and have in the process sensed the internal resonance of what you have written, then your message will come through with passion and conviction as you communicate. People will know what vision you propose, and will resonate with your character.

Composing the Guide might seem like a task to delegate. After all, unlike Matt Hyde, most people don't sit long nights in tents. I'm not suggesting that you must sit by a fire and compose every presentation or e-mail with a quill pen. I am suggesting that you must compose the broad range of the content of your conviction about what needs to change, even if the words are put to paper by someone else. I don't recommend surrogates for this task, but an interviewer could be helpful and you can use the questions posed in this book for that function. You must edit drafts from your own conviction, with your own stories and experience to maintain your independence. Writing your own conviction is like Woody Allen's characterization of taking a metaphysics final in college. You can't cheat by looking into the soul of the kid next to you.

Advisers can be very effective, but they have to be chosen carefully. The very best partners in this enterprise are not just good technicians; they are also strong thinkers and coaches who push you to articulate your own thoughts and feelings in the most effective way. Ted Sorenson, John Kennedy's speechwriter, was also Kennedy's chief of staff and conversed with the president every day. By contrast, many of today's communication professionals, while excellent composers, have little access to their principals. They may be able to predict the person's position or plan, but they know little of the inner drive or conviction of the person for whom they write. Any advisers you choose should be trusted associates whom you respect for more than their technical talent. They should also be willing to ask questions, push you to record your own thoughts and stories, offer substantive advice, and listen to you, and then reflect your own beliefs back to you in language that feels right to you, not only to them. You should take them into your confidence.

Mario Cuomo is a superb writer—yet he includes other associates in his process of constructing messages. In writing his remarks on abortion rights for the Department of Theology at the University of Notre Dame, he relied on two of his staff members: "gifted thinkers and writers, both of them profoundly Catholic and just as troubled as I was by the task of agonizing over the powerful, almost paralyzing issues raised by the abortion question. We wrote, discussed, debated, and finally decided."[1]

Not every communication opportunity will require you to use every element of your Guide. However, it will be the basis for most communication you have about your plan to change things for the better. Others can help, but finally, it is your own values, your own commitment to an issue that will determine the power of the message to you—and therefore to others. Whatever response you want from others must happen in you first. Working through the Guide will enable you to put the necessary leadership communication elements in place. In the process, you will increase your own clarity and deepen your conviction: you will be inspired to move ahead with the changes that are important to you.

These are the major sections of a Personal Leadership Communication Guide:

- Establishing Competence and Building Trustworthiness
- Creating Shared Context
- Declaring and Describing the Future
- Committing to Action

Each section includes specific sub-elements, each one contributing to the objectives of engaging yourself and others around the overall theme. The chapters devoted to each of these sections include many individual examples—some from clients, some from research—to demonstrate the principles. In addition, I use excerpts from two Guides as instructive examples for all of the elements. One is from a colleague and client leading a large organization. The other is a Guide that I've been developing for the last ten years regarding the primary and secondary education system in the United States.

Most people who read this work will have some opinion about education, wherever they reside. It is a worldwide issue and is administered in different ways in different cultures. Accordingly,

I suspect the topic will have some interest for everyone. Even so, there is danger in presenting this Guide. You might well disagree with some of the opinions expressed or find yourself distracted by the content. I hope this distraction does not occur and that even if your opinion on this issue differs from mine, you will see the power and content of the Guide's framework as demonstrated in a broad-gauged issue. If you wish to refer to the entire Guide, you can find it on the website (www.leadingoutloud.com).

As you prepare your own Guide, please remember that the sample Guides are offered only to model the form and the general content and flow. The next page presents the entire framework. This is replicated in Appendix B and at the website. Chapters Five through Eight follow with explanations, questions, and examples for each section.

Framework for Personal Leadership Communication Guide

1. Establishing Competence and Building Trustworthiness
    - Competence
        - Clarity of Purpose
          Problem
          Specific Change Advocated
          Evidence of Compelling Need
          Broad Implications, Value Represented
        - Credentials and Vulnerabilities
    - Trustworthiness
        - Displaying Empathy
          Expressing Gratitude
          Acknowledging Resistance
          Finding Commonality in Purpose
        - Willingness to Be Known
          Personal Motivation, Personal Value
2. Creating Shared Context
    - History
    - Priority
    - Current Reality (include barriers)
    - Reinforcing Competence and Trust
    - Articulating a Broader Perspective
3. Declaring and Describing the Future: An Act of Creation . . .
    - Vivid Picture, Sensory-Rich Images
    - Stakes (If we do . . . If we don't. . . .)
    - Values Expressed Either Way
4. Committing to Action
    - Steps (organizational)
    - Personal Commitment, Personal Action
    - Request for Action (specific)

Chapter Five

Establishing Competence and Building Trustworthiness

Any leader-inspired message for change must attend to three fundamental relationships—the relationship between the leader and the message, that between the leader and the constituents, and that between the constituents and the message. I have been addressing all three, emphasizing that the message has to be congruent with you as a person—the value represented by the change must be important to you.

The relationship you are trying to inspire is between other people and the message, so that people become committed to a cause voiced by you, the leader. Yet this commitment will happen only when the primary relationship, the one between you and those you hope to inspire, is based on your competence and trustworthiness. Quite naturally, these are the first considerations of anyone being asked to change, so the first section of the Leadership Communication Guide deals with these elements.

Establishing Competence

As you develop your Guide, you will need to answer a number of questions for yourself and then for others. The framework for the Guide starts with the elements that display competence: clear purpose and credentials.

Clarity of Purpose

- What is the problem?
- What is the specific change you are proposing?

- What one piece of evidence shows you and others a compelling need?
- What value is represented by the change and what are the broadest implications?

The answers to these questions will transform change into progress; they will support your advocacy and your zeal. Ignoring these questions instead of answering them for yourself first and then for others could send you on a vector that might well have a substantially different end point than you intended. Your answers to these questions will yield the grist to gain interest, to challenge others to act, to engage, to contribute. Unless they believe you know what you're doing and why, others might be entertained or bored, they might even be interested, but they will not engage with the message with any intent to act. For that engagement to occur, you need a clear idea of your purpose, one that is grounded in the practical necessity.

In 2013, we have the benefit of hindsight regarding the most challenging financial crisis of the last eighty years. Franklin Raines, former chairman and CEO of Fannie Mae, the primary real estate loan guarantor in the United States, is often maligned for his role in the fall of that institution. Yet, in the early 2000s, he carried a broad message that the African American effort for equality was not over. His purpose was, as he said in a 2002 speech to the Howard University graduating class, to "identify racial gaps," determine "why they exist," and determine "how we close them." What is the compelling need? According to Raines, "If America had racial equality in education, and jobs, African Americans would have . . . two million more high school degrees, two million more college degrees, . . . and nearly $200 billion more income." The disparity that exists, shown by the numbers, totals "over $1 trillion in wealth."[1] Problem: disparity. Purpose: cure it. Compelling evidence: clear. Specific Change: Make it possible for lower-income families to buy homes. To Raines's credit, he did not back down from his actions when called to a subcommittee of Congress in 2010. Perhaps he was overly zealous; perhaps he used a quasi-governmental agency to further a social goal. One could certainly discuss the effectiveness of his particular plan for progress or the wisdom of using public financing of homes to further social goals, but one could not question the purpose of his actions.

As with Franklin Raines, gaining clarity of purpose focuses your attention on your strongest conviction, and clarity of purpose focuses others' attention in a single direction. As it does, it begins to establish your own confidence, and others' feelings of confidence in you, the leader. Raines often spoke informally about the overriding vision of what he was trying to do. "We are in the American Dream Business," he would say, and one could certainly understand his enthusiasm as more and more people became qualified for home ownership.

Rebekah Saul Butler began to look at health care issues as a master's degree candidate at the University of California, Berkeley. She developed this statement of purpose to anchor her leadership effort in encouraging more conscious end-of-life decisions. Clearly, this states the evidence of the problem and the specific change she is after.

> End-of-life care is central to our national concern over the budget and the aging population, since 30 percent of all Medicare funds are spent in the last year of life. . . . I am going to advocate that we all have frank, open discussions in our families about these issues. . . . about aging, death and dying, what they mean, and how you will confront them.[2]

Clarity at the outset, even for a problem as daunting as death, serves notice to everyone that you are entering difficult territory with some courage behind your conviction. The more difficult the issue, the more clarity is needed. Rebekah's early work on her Guide became a precursor for her current work as a program director for a philanthropic foundation, in which she oversees the distribution of grants from the foundation in several related fields.

Authentic decisiveness creates respect. Others' disagreement with a leader on an issue can be countered by that leader's willingness to engage truthfully and boldly, so the more difficult the issue, the more desirable it is to be candid and forthright in formulating and stating your purpose. As a result of your strength, others will perceive a new possibility being created, and you will be marked as a person of principle and a person of strong conviction; people will perceive you as a person of competence.

Political leaders know this principle well, and generally get their point of view out very early in any communication. Consider the first sentence of the text of the late Senator Edward Kennedy's prepared speech on Iraq in late 2002: "I have come here today to express my view that America should not go to war against Iraq unless and until other reasonable alternatives are exhausted."[3]

Clarity and strength of purpose help establish competence, and compel others to engage. They do not commit you to inflexibility but do establish your desire to engage.

I offer here the first elements of a Guide I've been working on since 2003; it is now in its fifteenth update. I've used this Guide more than a hundred times in advocating change in the education system in the United States, in many different venues.

Sample from the Education Guide

Purpose: This guide proposes a fundamental change in our system of primary and secondary education in the United States.

Specific Change: We should focus our efforts and most of our educational resources on retaining the teachers who are passionate and effective in their work, and in developing these characteristics in new recruits to teach.

Compelling Need and Evidence: We need reform because our federal and state governments are, in general, not being effective at improving our system. Our federal government's effort at supporting education is, as SAT CEO Gaston Caperton once said, "like making a bread sandwich"—standards on one side and measurement (testing) on the other, with no nourishment in the middle—nothing to support students to actually grow from inadequate to outstanding in their achievement. Our state efforts are generally focused on things that, according to new research, don't matter much, like administration, formal teacher certification, reducing class size (to the exclusion of everything else), and specific curriculum. According to the Justice Department, in 1993, 20 percent of high school graduates could not read their diploma. By 2011, there were 3.1 million students graduating. If that rate is consistent, more than half a million of them could not handle the complexity of that small document, and this, of course, does not account for the dropouts, also a substantial number.

Broadest Implication and Value Represented: This is about *fairness*. If a system is going to be public, it should deliver fair value to all, not just to an elite few. Yet this bifurcation has happened despite the fact that most of us believe that a basic education is fundamental to participative democracy. A nation that shows no commitment to broad-based education is doomed to failure as the population becomes, on the average, less sophisticated, less knowledgeable, and less able to care for itself. This not only erodes our place in the world, it creates decay from within, cheapening our heritage and creating grave doubts about our future.

We need to reverse this trend.

This opening of the Guide establishes its foundation and urgency. I revise the evidentiary elements as new data becomes available. The issue is clear.

The next questions have to do with your capability and interest in leading change.

Credentials and Vulnerability

- What work experience, life experience, and education qualify you to lead change in this area?
- What are your vulnerabilities?

Your competence to lead a given change with a given group is a function of your directly relevant work experience, life experience, and education, as well as additional credentials that might be important to the particular constituency. If you have the title of leader you might well have the formal authority to lead, but to follow your lead with their own commitment, people will need to know how you gained competence in your chosen field.

Many of us underplay our credentials, either out of modesty or from the common tendency to believe that others should just know our background. But would you consider following the lead of anyone whose credentials you don't know? As you develop your Guide, you do have to consider your qualifications and be clear about them. Remember, the Guide is a tool for you to use to engage, so while you will mention different parts of it in any given communication, you want to include every relevant bit of experience and education in the Guide itself—particularly those items that are especially meaningful to you and that might be meaningful to someone else. You then need to find a way to make your constituents aware of the qualifications they would find particularly important—those that would give them confidence in your ability.

You also need to consider *doubts* others might have and acknowledge your own gaps in credentials. The authenticity of disclosing vulnerabilities builds trust, inevitably preventing or mitigating attacks in the future. It also allows you to be realistic, to assess what other help you will need for the implementation. As you begin to communicate you will encounter others who will fill those gaps in your own ability. At the very least, even if you never *disclose* these vulnerabilities, you want to make sure you are aware of them. Someone will probably bring them up. They belong in your Guide.

While he was governor of New York, Mario Cuomo was a champion of abortion rights as a matter of public policy—but he was also a practicing, devout Catholic. As hinted at in Part Two's opening text, when he was asked to address the combined faculty and administration of Notre Dame on the subject, he found it the perfect opportunity to think through and ferret out his own logic and feeling on this subject in a way that he had not before. The address that he eventually gave formed the basis for his extemporaneous remarks on the subject of the relationship of his faith to his public policy for the rest of his career. Considering the audience for this particular speech, and his constituents in general, he felt the need to tell them directly who he was and who he was not. Try to put yourself in this audience as he addresses this issue:

> Let me begin this part of the effort by underscoring the obvious. I do not speak as a theologian; I do not have that competence. I do not speak as a philosopher; to suggest that I could would be to set a new record for false pride. I don't presume to speak as a "good" person except in the ontological sense of that word. [Rather], I speak here as a politician. And also as a Catholic, a layperson baptized and raised in the pre-Vatican II church, educated in Catholic schools, attached to the church first by birth, then by choice, now by love. An old-fashioned Catholic who sins, regrets, struggles, worries, gets confused, and most of the time feels better after confession. The Catholic church is my spiritual home. My heart is there, and my hope.[4]

Would you have listened, despite any disagreement with his position as you knew it? Aside from the beautiful words, the content of this supplementary self-introduction did far more for Cuomo's trustworthiness with this group and the millions who have viewed or read it since than the bulk of the message. This passage was far more important than the fact that he was a governor who wrestled with public policy every day. He established his connection with this audience as a human being by including his personal motivation to speak and his personal vulnerabilities. Despite the fact that he was advocating a very unpopular position with this group, he was going to be trusted.

Cultural Differences in Credentials

In each culture there are certain credentials that are considered fundamental to one's ability to lead. These may seem superficial, but in the early stages of a change effort, before others have had a chance to evaluate what you say or to hear your conviction on the subject, you need to establish a foothold of competence, just to open the group's collective mind to your leadership. In Europe, family history, social standing, and education are generally considered more important than in the United States, where life experience—what you've done on your own—will be considered as important as your alma mater. In Asia, credentials are often established by family and in some subtler way, to avoid the leader being perceived as self-serving.

Groups of people engaged in specific professions will also demand different evidence to demonstrate competence. An academic group will indeed be interested in your academic credentials, even if they are not directly related to the project. When I was teaching at UC Berkeley in the late 1980s, a dean was appointed who was from the business community. Charged with the monumental task of building a new school, he struggled with lackluster respect from the faculty because he was not an academic. But he had the exact skills and connections to enable him to complete the construction of one of the most beautiful and functional buildings on campus. The constituents who mattered—those who provided the funds—were happy to have him at the helm.

If you are leading a business group to take more risk, then work or life experience is far more valuable than academics in establishing credibility. Bill Gates's and Mark Zuckerberg's work experience are certainly adequate to establish their competence, despite the fact that neither graduated from college. They are not alone. John Bunch, largely responsible for the growth of TD Ameritrade to become a major player in brokerage, does not have a college degree, but he was instrumental in the ascent of Charles Schwab into the realm of integrated web and personal service brokerage. He is currently CEO of a registered investment advisory firm, which may under his leadership shift the method of buying mutual funds in the United States.

Central to the point is that our history gives us a peek at what we will contribute. When we are young, we are attracted to what we love, and if we are lucky, following that urge yields a career.

A few years ago, a young environmentalist named Rob Nicholson was developing a Communication Guide to lead his peers in conservation. In preparing the base message, he included this statement of credentials:

> I have been extremely fortunate to have spent most of my life educating myself for my work. I have spent almost twenty-five years in schools and over thirty years in the outdoors. I've traveled from the Arctic Ocean to the Equator, climbed some of the highest peaks in Europe and trekked through the

> jungles of Borneo. As an environmental consultant for six years, I've visited more garbage dumps than I care to remember. I've been involved with oil spills off the coast of Alaska and train wrecks in densely populated urban areas.

His conclusion from all these experiences was that we are not living a sustainable existence and have to change the way we relate to our environment.

Nicholson's notations of credentials were not arrogant or self-serving. By formulating them, he was able to feel more powerful about the topic as he prepared to simply and colorfully let others know what life experience, education, and work experience was relevant to his committed course of change. He intentionally referred to himself as "extremely fortunate," because he really felt that way. In the process of relating his experience, he did not set himself above others. Instead, the wording he chose reflected his real humility, beginning to move him toward a deeper connection with his work and with others he hoped would participate.

The next excerpt from my Education Leadership Communication Guide addresses this issue.

Sample from the Education Guide

Credentials and Vulnerabilities: Now I think I need to reveal to you the obvious. . . . I am not Joseph Chilton Pearce, the great American educational guru—I am Terry Pearce. I only recently earned a master's degree, and it's in mythology, not education. I graduated from a small university in the state of Oregon and did some limited graduate work in the field of law. I am probably also vulnerable to a charge of being anti-bureaucrat, and I realize that my experience is not everyone's experience.

However, I have been involved in education as a teacher for the past twenty years, all of it at the graduate level in professional business schools and schools of public policy and private development companies. This is not my full-time vocation, but it is my love. Every day, I hear the concerns of

(*Continued*)

graduate students and executives, and by any measure, the quality of public education is their number one issue, as they strive to recruit and retain employees, and to market to an ever-less-discerning public. I have actually helped politicians "dumb-down" messages for fear that an uneducated public simply can't grasp the subtleties necessary to make an informed choice.

As a student, parent of three, and grandparent of six, I've been exposed to the public school system directly for sixty-five years, and that experience also informs my desire to be involved.

Beginning the Guide with thoughtfulness about your purpose, the specifics of the change, a striking bit of evidence, and the broader implications and values involved will establish your purpose and the primary facts and impressions that are driving your conviction. It will also move you forward as you document the basis of your own excitement and passion for the change. Sharing your credentials and vulnerabilities will align you with the people you are engaging. This is all about competence. The issue of trust comes next, and it's somewhat harder to tackle.

Building Trust—Authenticity

With your competence established through clarity and credentials, you can move toward thinking through and documenting the elements that will establish your trustworthiness. We trust other people when we believe we know who they are at the core and that they authentically have our best interest at heart. The operative word is *authentically.* If you really don't care about others, if you have no urge or instinct to acknowledge them as you encourage change, you will not be able to gain their trust, even if you follow verbal conventions. As explained in Chapter Two, we all have a built-in ability to decipher intention, though in some this ability is solely unconscious. People know when you care about them.

Without caring, trust conventions are simply rituals that sound good but no longer facilitate connection. These conventions were at one time meaningful, but have since become formalities that we follow (usually unconsciously) to avoid real contact. As but one example, how many times have you heard or participated in this exchange?

"May I help you?"

"No thanks, I'm just looking."

Retail chains spend millions to get rid of this conventional conversation. In 2000, Safeway instituted a policy that required checkout personnel to offer customers help to their cars and to call them by name, a policy that was ignored or openly mocked by many employees—and deeply offensive to many customers. Rules such as these can help accomplish the objective only if there is agreement that such proposed practices indeed include the best interest of employees. If a leader advocates a culture of service and personal connection and can point accurately to its benefit to the entire employee base, then workers will not only cooperate with the policy, they will improve it, fix it, make suggestions about it, and engage fully in its implementation. Conversely, if the leader is seen the same way as Dilbert might see the pointy-headed boss—as a manipulative self-serving bureaucrat—then there is little chance of real change. In the ensuing twelve years, Safeway seems to have turned the credibility corner and other chain stores are emulating them. Inspiration is key. If the people staffing the checkout stands really want to serve, really want to connect, they will do so with no rules. Yet if retail salespeople aren't really interested in helping, that will come through without regard to what they say.

Building trust assures that you have the best interest of everyone at heart, and creates the atmosphere for change initiatives of yours to be taken seriously, whether the constituents are members of organized labor, freelancers, or your family. A loss of trust undermines all else. Two CEOs in the powerful Silicon Valley were dismissed in 2010 to 2012 for what their boards considered breaches of trust. Scott Thompson was ousted at Yahoo after being accused of overstating his education, and Mark Hurd left Hewlett-Packard under duress after the board discovered the appearance of impropriety in a high-level consulting contract.

Neither of these men could be described as lacking competence, yet both gave the appearance of a lack of trustworthiness.

Trustworthiness, authentic trustworthiness, appears in many forms and can be undermined in still more. People often use conventional words of acknowledgment to get over the initial anxiety of meeting. A speaker may start by saying, "It's wonderful to be here tonight." Auditors may start by saying, "We're here to help," and the person being audited may reply, "I'm glad to see you." If you avoid using these and similar conventions, and instead enter into the relationship consciously, you can signal your intention to interact more authentically. I can illustrate.

In 1983, I was fortunate enough to meet with former president Jimmy Carter in Beverly Hills, California. My business partner Tom and I were promoting a very simple plan to relieve political tension between the United States and the Soviet Union. Carter had agreed to a short meeting to hear about it.

A Secret Service agent ushered us into the suite; Carter entered briskly shortly thereafter. Since Tom was standing closer to him, he shook Carter's hand first and said something like, "I am honored to meet you, Mr. President. You have been a real inspiration to me." Carter looked right at him and said, "Oh really, Tom, how's that?" I quickly ducked my head and waited for my partner to come up with something good, and in that painful ten seconds of silence that seemed like a day and a half, I learned a valuable lesson about appreciation. If it's authentic, it's written on your heart by experience, not on a piece of paper by convention. My partner's comment was real, he just had not reflected on *why* it was real.

Tom made a nice recovery, saying something about Carter's obvious deep partnership with Rosalyn and his courage in running for the presidency against heavy odds. When Carter shook my hand, I did not offer a gratuitous comment.

How many leaders could pass muster when facing a question like Carter's? Imagine the host of a party stopping you after you have said, "What a lovely home," with the comment, "Oh really, Tom, how's that?"

Once you learn how to stay real, you are able to acknowledge others authentically rather than conventionally. In doing so, a leader can establish uncommon intimacy very quickly. Affirmation of others, or caring, is central to building trust, and includes the ability to express gratitude and empathize with others' points of view. You must also being willing to be known—to reveal your personal motivations.

Displaying Empathy

- What am I truly thankful for, with regard to this chance to communicate or to those I will interact with?
- On whose shoulders do I stand?
- What are people likely to be thinking and feeling about this issue?
- What emotional and mental resistance will others have to this change?

Steve Farber, author of *Greater Than Yourself* and an exceptional coach and speaker, frequently asks his audiences: "How many of you have ever received a note from someone expressing sincere appreciation?" Most in the audience will raise their hands. "How many of you still have that note?" Most will keep their hands up. He then asks how long the members of the audience have kept the notes. "Five years?" "Ten years?" Many hands remain up even as Steve asks, "Twenty-five years?" But the record is *forty* years, and when Steve asked his respondent if he remembered what the note said, the person reached into his pocket and pulled the note from his wallet. After forty years, he still considered it one of his most prized possessions.

Have you kept a similar note? And if you have, what is your opinion and feeling about the person who wrote it?

These are not rhetorical questions. The ability and willingness to express sincere appreciation is one of the most valuable skills of leadership communication. People will be inclined to follow others who make them feel good about themselves, who display an honest appreciation for who they are and what they do for the organization. As a leader, why not ask yourself what you are truly thankful for, with regard to every chance to communicate? Who—and what circumstance—can you authentically acknowledge as a gift? Whose shoulders do you stand on?

Expressing Gratitude

It sounds simple, yet as the story of the thank-you notes shows, the expression of sincere gratitude is rare and valuable. It is not easy to convey authentic appreciation; moreover, it is not considered important in a world where convention rather than authenticity rules most human communication.

A few years ago, I was attending a program conducted by Brother David Steindl-Rast, a Benedictine monk and a prolific writer on gratefulness, a wonderful teacher, and a person I count as a rare, authentic human being. Brother David described an exercise that one of his teachers had prescribed for him as he was trying to understand gratitude. "For one year," said the abbot, "I want you to write two notes of gratitude before you leave your room in the morning." "Easy enough," thought Brother David, until the teacher added, "and you have to experience the gratitude!"

Brother David is now known worldwide for his pioneering and relentless commitment to gratitude as the key to successful living. His organization (A Network for Grateful Living), website (www.gratefulness.org), writings, and personal appearances reach millions of people every year.

We all know how to say "thank you," just as we know how to say "may I help you," yet few of us consider—in the way Brother David does—how to generate the experience of being grateful. Unfortunately, unless we do generate that experience in ourselves, the object of our thanks will experience only the conventional and obligatory communication—"Thanks"—hardly a note worth keeping for forty years.

Leaders can develop the capability of generating the experience of gratitude in themselves in order to engender the kind of loyalty displayed by those who keep notes for forty years. I've tried the "don't leave your room until you feel grateful" exercise myself. It is enlightening, and en-heartening. Should you try it, you will find that real gratitude is accessed from experience, not from rhetoric. Experience brings with it specificity and feelings, both generators of an authentic response.

A friend and client, the late Ned Dean, was chairman of the Pacific Bank in San Francisco. He wanted to acknowledge one of his board members at a stockholders' meeting at the end of a difficult two years. After he wrote several iterations that used conventional language, I asked Ned to be more specific and detailed. He wrote the following, and later conveyed it to his stockholders. Nearly twenty years later, his expression of gratitude remains one of the best I've ever heard:

> I want to give special thanks to Mark Hubbard, who attended more than fifty board and committee meetings last year, strictly out of his dedication to helping us turn the situation around. I remember one such occasion, about seven o'clock at night in the dead of winter, when I was leaving my office as Mark was coming in. He had just finished a day at his own company, and it was raining, a cold rain that would turn to snow in any other city. He had forgotten his umbrella, so his head was soaked as he came into the lobby. I actually felt guilty leaving so early. Now it's not as though Mark doesn't have other interests. He came to that meeting because he is dedicated, more as a friend of the company than as a board member. And he did it more than fifty times when we needed him most. I feel very lucky to have such friends serving all of us.

By reflecting on his specific experience, Ned was able to access real gratitude, not merely talk about conceptual gratitude. His authenticity moved the audience, Hubbard, and Ned himself, with more than information.

Karen Chang had a similar experience in conveying gratitude for her group of senior vice presidents of Charles Schwab. These were people who had traveled extensively in the previous year, moving from branch to branch in a major change effort. Karen could have merely said, "I want to particularly express my appreciation to the senior vice presidents for their tireless efforts and extensive travel this last year." By convention, that would be acceptable. Rather than staying with convention, Karen did a bit of research and conveyed her feelings this way. "I want to particularly thank the senior vice presidents who made this happen by being on the road. They were gone from their homes an average of fifteen nights a month last year. All of them have families; and believe me, I know that 174 nights is a lot of nights to go to bed without a hug from someone you love. I deeply appreciate them and their families for that."

Magic. She reflected, included herself, was specific, and made it real. Her feelings were obvious, as were the feelings of everyone else in the room. By conveying feelings that came from a real experience, she made the entire episode reflect what she wanted to reflect.

Learning to express authentic gratitude is central to leadership communication and perhaps, as Brother David suggests, a key to living in fullness. Seeking gratitude in the everyday can be enriching to everyone, including you, the leader. Here is an excerpt from the Guide on education. My question was: "Who am I truly grateful for with regard to the education system?"

Sample from the Education Guide

Gratitude: One thing I can say for sure is that I would not be in the position that I am in had I not had the benefit of a couple of great teachers; and in my time, they indeed came out of this public system. I am eternally grateful for their influence in shaping who I am today. My third-grade teacher, Helen Stroup, was a paragon of a self-esteeming woman, and would accept nothing less than my best, even challenging me to a personal race through the times-tables in front of the room. My early mathematics teacher in high school, Ted Thebe, showed enough faith in me to raise my own expectations of what I could do . . . not just in math, but in life, entering me in math contests and helping me prepare on weekends. I'm sure that many people that I will speak to about reform have shared similar experiences and are grateful for them.. My own mother, who only had a high-school education, nonetheless believed in the value of as much education as one could get. It was her focus and persuasion that made it possible for me to be the first and only member of my family to go to university and beyond, something not common in her generation.

Acknowledging Resistance

Your expressions of authentic gratitude will help others recognize your humanity, but might do little to give them an experience of your empathy with their own points of view. Resistance and disagreement are natural responses to a call for change. Before making that call, you need to consider what people might be thinking and feeling about this issue. You need to consider what their natural mental and emotional resistance to this change might be, and be ready to acknowledge this resistance in advance. In very real terms, this is "empathy in advance"—it is a chance to consider others before you actually encounter them. As you know, people don't like change, and at first mention, lacking context or further explanation, they will resist, even if they don't show it.

In business lore of the 1950s, Alfred Sloan, head of General Motors, was purportedly in a board meeting, about to make an important decision. He said, "I take it that everyone is in basic agreement with this decision." Everyone nodded. Sloan looked at the group and said, "Then I suggest we postpone the decision. Until we have some disagreement, we don't understand the problem."[5] Of course he was right. Often, resistance will remain silent unless the leader is sensitive and smart enough to acknowledge it up front. When it is acknowledged, resistance can be a powerful building block for eventual agreement and engagement. As you build your Guide, considering other points of view and possible objections is important to your being able to think through the cogency of your own ideas. More important, it is central to being able to acknowledge others' ideas and feelings as a way of building trust.

Of course, most of us fail to do this. We think through others' arguments, but we define them only as hurdles that we have to knock down or leap over to get our own way, rather than the reasonable points of view of others we hope to lead into a relationship of trust. Jim Nunan, a friend, client, and long-time high-level HR executive, told me a story about one of his general managers who'd been the focus of a series of complaints from employees. While the complaints varied in intensity, the subject matter was always the same—the executive did not listen. Jim made an appointment to speak to the executive about the problem and arrived at the appointed time.

He began to spell out the problem, and noticed that as he spoke, the executive was making notes on the pad on his desk. "This is impressive," mused Jim. "He's writing down what I'm saying. It doesn't look like a lack of listening to me." Just then the executive was called from the room to take a phone call. Quickly, Jim looked at the notes. The GM had not been taking notes—he had been writing down his rebuttal.

Most of us are actively thinking about rebuttal, even if we are not making notes. If you are a change agent, your strong statements of purpose will amplify feelings and ideas of resistance in others, and will probably provoke expressions of discontent. These contrary ideas and feelings of discontent are present whether you acknowledge them or not. By bringing them to the surface, you establish your ability to be empathetic, and you demonstrate your willingness to become a partner rather than an adversary. By shining light on these thoughts and feelings early, you maintain and reinforce your motivation. In fact, recognizing resistance as normal gives you yet another chance to create real limbic resonance with others, to connect with their hearts, not just their minds.

Conversely, if you pretend that acceptance of your new proposal will come without uncertainty, you will lose your credibility. You risk being undermined—and you will never gain the full commitment of others. They may comply, but their resistance will manifest itself in negativity and an absence of energy for the task at hand. Resistance not acknowledged will continue to thrive, not only as others listen to your comments, but also in the halls, bathrooms, cars, and homes where people say what has not been said in your presence. By acknowledging resistance, you are acknowledging reality.

I first heard of this idea from Harvey Stone, a speech coach and writer in Santa Fe, New Mexico. Harvey used the example of a domestic discussion, in which a couple is in a heated exchange, sometimes for days, until one of them (Harvey says it is most often his wife) acknowledges the other's feelings and opinions. Imagine yourself in a combative mood, as your adversary stops, pauses, and says: "You know, I didn't realize that you felt so strongly about this issue. You sound as though you feel hurt, and I know that you honestly disagree with my point of view."

There is no agreement in this statement, only honest noticing and honoring of some strong feelings and a different opinion. While the discussion certainly isn't over, one can feel the adverse energy drain out of the situation, so that ears might be open to hear for the first time in the "discussion." This same release occurs whenever negative feelings and opinions are acknowledged. The respect voiced by the leader for other points of view can open the minds of dissenters as the leader's motivation becomes less suspect. Such acknowledgment does not *guarantee* agreement with your position, but it will dissipate the argumentative energy and open the possibility of honest dialogue.

Rational Resistance and Cynicism

The easiest resistance to suspend is based on different or less knowledge. The leader simply has information that others do not have. Others may be cynical about the proposed change because they think it has been tried before, or they may be fearful of change because of their lack of knowledge. Such resistance can be considered and acknowledged in the beginning of any message. It can be refuted later if need be, but in the spirit of common understanding rather than argument.

What does this look like?

In developing a Guide for a change in supply chain management, John Ure was suggesting a new focus on customers, a holistic approach that would create an integration of the supply chain. He made the following notes about resistance:

> When thinking about this new way, I can hear voices, my own included, that argue, from Marketing, "I already focus on the customer, although perhaps not to the point of actual intimacy, so why the need to change?" Or from Purchasing, "I have already developed excellent partnership with our suppliers, why do we need to change?" Or from Design, "Don't come and tell me how to design a product; I am perfectly competent, so just get on with getting the best price." Indeed we do all of those things, and I don't want to lose this focus, this partnership, or this competency in design.

These notes on resistance do not, in themselves, refute the resistance. They merely help John and others know that he was under no illusions about their point of view. In fact, he acknowledged his own resistance at the same time ("my own included"). When these other players realized that John knew about their doubts and was open to them, they were, in kind, open to hear what else he had to say, and they were willing to engage with him, knowing that he could acknowledge their point of view.

As we've seen, resistance can be a matter of feeling as well as a matter of differences between ideas or intellectual doubts—it can come from uneasiness with whoever the leader seems to be. There were four debates in the 2012 U.S. presidential election cycle. In the first, the President was described as "listless, smirking, demeaning, and seeming to be intellectually superior," while his opponent was seen as "aggressive, assertive, and confident." The vice-presidential debate was described by a CNN reporter as "really great television" because the candidates were animated and argumentative. Still, the vice president frequently mimicked his opponent by interrupting with "blah, blah, blah"—brash, disrespectful, and arrogant.

Resistance is not always conscious, and in fact is frequently created by just such subtle actions or impressions. It was not hard for me to imagine that the vice-presidential debate was a mirror of what goes on in the U.S. Congress every day—the disrespectful and overbearing expressing of polarized opinions in a polarizing way. It is no wonder that very little is accomplished.

Resistance based on a different or inadequate understanding of the facts can be relieved with explanation. John Ure went on to address the resistance later in his Guide, by explaining the difference in his new plan and the status quo, using common metaphors to educate others and assuage their fears.

Irrational Resistance—Feelings

Other resistance comes not from any lack of understanding but from just plain fear of change. Tom Haverty runs Bioventures for Merck, one of the world's premier drug manufacturers. He is known for his ability to communicate authentically, and told me in a recent interview that he has had this ability since the fourth grade. "I don't think of the audience's head. I ask myself, 'Where are they emotionally—what would I be thinking if I were in their shoes?' Then I address that issue first."

I asked Tom if he is a good listener, and he said yes. We sparred for a minute about "understanding content," and "feeling heard." His distinction was between the two French verbs *écouter* (to listen) and *entendre* (to attend)—exactly the point. As Tom pointed out, giving full attention is quite different from merely hearing words.

The next selection from the Education Guide shows the treatment of resistance.

Sample from the Education Guide

Resistance: I understand that there is not enough money to implement every idea, and that shifting major resources to encourage teachers like my own heroes and heroines will come at the expense of those who teach mostly because it is a safe profession with summers off. And I know how threatening a basic change like this can seem, especially to those who have a vested interest in the status quo—many of whom are doing their best to accomplish the same end that I have in mind.

Some who have worked at reform all of their lives might see this idea as simplistic. Some might feel threatened or unappreciated, and others might just think that I am a real outsider who doesn't understand the system. Truly, many before me, and perhaps better qualified, have had turns at reform.

Of course, I will mention the teachers' unions in this message many times, and while I will note some of the negative impact of the unions on the schools, I realize that much of their activity has been positive and indeed necessary to protect the labor rights of teachers. I also recognize

(*Continued*)

that unions themselves have made significant contribution to the capability of many kids to be able to go to school at all.

Finally, some might hear some of what I have to offer as an indictment of the entire system and be offended by that. Believe me, I understand that feeling. It is hard not to generalize, yet I recognize that there are pockets of excellence in the greater pile of what others might call mediocrity.

Commonality

- What do all the constituents in this change share in common?

Just as acknowledging resistance states our differences—what might draw us apart—commonality synthesizes, it brings us together. Around any change, commonality calls for hope and conviction that we all want the same outcome—only our methods, time line, and perhaps the volume of resources to be devoted to that outcome are different. It is important to acknowledge the common objective, bringing everyone into the same tent, despite fears, despite different ideas and beliefs. This can be a very large tent, as it was for John Kennedy as he defined commonality during his 1963 speech at American University, where he laid out his own belief that world peace was not beyond our grasp: "For, in the final analysis, our most basic common link is that we all inhabit this small planet. We all breathe the same air. We all cherish our children's future. And we are all mortal."[6]

Kennedy uses the broadest commonality—humankind—and the result was immortality for his words. For the Guide on education, not as universal, I wrote the paragraph in the next excerpt.

Sample from the Education Guide

Commonality: So I approach this with optimism. I know that while everyone might not agree on the means to the end, we all share the desire for the system to be as robust and effective as possible. Like you, I want the best outcome, the most efficient system, and a renewal of true "public" education, where individuals can count on a level of knowledge and behavior that is consistent, fairly applied, and inspiring. I hope that this discussion is a part of the impetus for meaningful action.

As new questions are asked, as new objections and resistance present themselves, as new commonality becomes apparent, this section is enlarged and clarified, and it becomes more nuanced—all with the same end—not to appear to listen (*écouter*) but to really hear (*entendre*).

Willingness to Be Known: Personal Motivation

- Why does this issue matter to me personally?
- What personal experience or story could demonstrate my conviction?
- What core principle, value, or belief is represented by this change?
- What is it that I stand for in this situation?

To agree to act, people want to know why a change is important to the organization and how they will benefit, but to commit to follow a leader down an uncertain path, they have to know the leader's personal motivation—it is central to trustworthiness. It doesn't have to do with material outcome, it has to do with meaning. "I have a dream," was Martin Luther King's personal motivation. Examining your own motivation and revealing it is part of building trust.

The best example I've ever heard of this aspect of earning trust was brought to my attention by Peter Alduino, a leadership consultant from Santa Cruz and author of *The Citizen Leader.* I grant you that this example is dated, but I have found none more elegant. Peter located a videotape, made in 1974, of the late Barbara Jordan. Jordan, an African American, was then a member of the U.S. House of Representatives from Texas, and on the tape was speaking to the committee hearing the evidence to impeach former President Nixon. As a junior member of the committee, she spoke for fifteen minutes, including this prologue:

> Earlier today, we heard the beginning to the preamble to the Constitution of the United States . . . "we the people," a very eloquent beginning. But when that document was completed on the seventeenth of September in 1787, I was not included in "we the people."
>
> I felt somehow for many years that George Washington and Alexander Hamilton just left me out by mistake. But through the process of amendment, interpretation, and court decision, I have finally been included in "we the people."
>
> Today I am an inquisitor, and hyperbole would not be fictional and would not overstate the solemnness that I feel right now. My faith in the Constitution is whole, it is complete, it is total. And I am not going to sit here and be an idle spectator to the diminution, the subversion, the destruction of the Constitution.[7]

There is no question about Jordan's personal motivation, why it matters to her personally, the core principles at stake, and what she stands for. Her personal experience, like the beginning to the Constitution's preamble, is elegant. Any constituent who felt equally disenfranchised or felt strongly about equality would be inspired by her statement. Notice that it is personal, not theoretical. Jordan did not say, "Everyone should be diligent in protecting the constitution, because it is the basis of our freedom as a nation." Although she certainly would agree with that statement, her personal motivation is what creates the platform for her very personal leadership on this issue.

One of the most intelligent and globally insightful executives I've ever worked with is Nick Roelofs, president of Agilent's Life

Sciences Group. Nick was a true prodigy and had the privilege of meeting and speaking with a number of Nobel Prize winners at a very young age. In working with him as he developed a Guide for his enterprise, I asked what got him into this business. He said, "At one point I realized that I was probably not going to win a Nobel Prize—and I decided I wanted to build tools for those who would." I encouraged him, with some success, to tell that to others, to consider it as part of his Personal Leadership Communication Guide. When he first shared it, people remembered it, because it is true, it is reflective, it is personal, and it is inspiring.

Meaning is conveyed when we can connect our actions to our personal values. Sometimes that is done with a story, as it was with me as I realized the connection between delivering kids to college and delegation. The experience made delegation meaningful to me, just as Barbara Jordan's very intense personal experience made the health of the Constitution meaningful to her.

Many might think that this connection can't be made in a business environment, but consider the story of Howard Schultz that I related in Chapter One. Schultz was very clear about his personal motivation for building Starbucks into the kind of company it is, where everyone feels like a partner. His experience with his father drove his values to the surface, and he was able to express them later in his business. Schultz's revelation carried with it not only his personal motivation but the aura of vulnerability that brings others close.

The next selection presents what is in the education Leadership Communication Guide for personal motivation.

Sample from the Education Guide

Personal Motivation: I can tell you that my initial impetus for studying this problem was sheer frustration. In my life as a parent, I have sat through countless school board meetings, voted for millions in taxes, volunteered in libraries, and I've even been the only single father who functioned as a third-grade teacher's aide.

(*Continued*)

I've also had one son nearly fall through the substantial cracks of the public system, largely because of my misplaced faith and lack of understanding. . . . He never had the privilege of a Mrs. Stroup . . . not once in his nine years in the public program. Had he not been so responsible and assertive about it, or if we had not decided to fund his future in a private school, he might not have ever known that he was capable of Dean's List work, he might not have been admitted to the University of California, and might not have gone on to success in business and life. In the space of three years at that small private school he was blessed with three great teachers. . . . Yes, he had larger class sizes, and he had less than current curriculum, but he had three great teachers. They made all the difference, and of course they were paid less than their counterparts in the public system. They taught there because they loved education and hated bureaucracy.

When my oldest son was a senior in a public high school, the honors English teacher offered an evening class in creative writing, not just for honors students, but to anyone who wanted to sign up. As an enhancement she required that a parent had to take the class with the student. More than eighty kids and parents signed up, and her first assignment was for each of us to write a poem about our father. I was close to my son already, but I can tell you that in the course of those thirteen weeks, we talked about more things that were important than ever before or since, and many parents and children talked to one another as they never had . . . and of course, everyone learned to write. The teacher had conceived a wonderful class, and only her own passion allowed it to happen . . . in the evening.

That class only lasted two years. I was told it was because the union would not allow her to extend her day, even as she wanted to. Yet in California alone last year we spent 80 percent of our education budget on things that the union supports, primarily class size control to require more teachers sharing less money. In the meantime, this teacher has moved on. The cancellation of this evening class was surely not the only reason, yet students and parents who might have benefited have lost a remarkable teacher.

Based upon just these two examples, you can by now feel the strength of my personal motivation.

***

Clear purpose, credentials and vulnerability, personal motivation, expressing gratitude, acknowledging others' points of view . . . these and more are all aspects of a leadership communication that you need to ponder and record before you move into the issue itself. Of course, these are all aspects of emotional intelligence, and your willingness to consider them supports your decision to lead, not just dictate, change.

Your relationship to those you hope to inspire, and your relationship to the message you hope to deliver, have to be clear and deep for you to be perceived as an authentic leader, both competent and personally trustworthy. Once you have completed this thinking, you have a chance of gaining real, committed support. The beginning of the Guide sets the tone and the limits for you and those you wish to engage, inviting them to entertain change. The degree of both confidence and trust that develops between you and others will be determined by the authenticity of the beliefs you can access, record, and later transmit under a myriad circumstances. The tone of your credentials, the way in which you show appreciation for your listeners, the strength of your purpose, the empathy you portray for their resistance, and the cost and benefit they perceive in your advocacy—each of these elements will affect their willingness to engage.

After you have included these rudiments, you need to record your perspective of the history and present in a story that compels you to seek change at all, to seek *this* change in particular, and to seek it now.

Questions to Ask in Establishing Competence and Building Trust Worthiness

- Competence
  - Clarity of Purpose:
    - What is the problem?
    - What is the specific change you are proposing?
    - What one piece of evidence shows you and others a compelling need?
    - What value is represented by the change and what are the broadest implications?
  - Credentials and Vulnerabilities
    - What work experience, life experience, and education qualify you to lead change in this area?
    - What are my vulnerabilities?
      - What is it that I don't know?
      - What are the areas in which I don't yet have expertise with regard to this issue?
      - What help will I need?
      - What mistakes might I have made with regard to this issue or with this group that I could acknowledge?
      - What obstacles are in this for me personally?
- Trustworthiness
  - Displaying Empathy
    - Gratitude
      - What am I truly thankful for, with regard to this chance to communicate or those I will interact with?
      - Who and what circumstances can I authentically acknowledge as a gift?
      - On whose shoulders do I stand?
    - Acknowledging Resistance and Commonality
      - What emotional and mental resistance will others have to this change?
      - What do all the constituents in this change share in common?
      - What aspirations do we share?

Personal Motivation/Personal Values

- Why does this issue matter to me personally?
- What personal experience or story could demonstrate my conviction?
- What core principle, value, or belief is represented by this change?
- What is it that I stand for in this situation?

Chapter Six

Creating Shared Context

"All truth passes through three stages. . . . First it is ridiculed, second it is violently opposed, third it is accepted as being self-evident." This comment is variously attributed to eighteenth-century philosopher Arthur Schopenhauer, George Bernard Shaw, and Mahatma Gandhi. Like most aphorisms, if measured against great changes in history, it would seem to be true. Change occurs when it is time. A leader notices that history has pointed the way toward change and, by skillful and heartfelt communication, makes the direction of change obvious to others. Where we've been points to where we are, which points to where we are going. Yet as things shift, others see either change, progress, or both, depending literally on their point of view. What they perceive as past and future and how they perceive your competence and trustworthiness will largely determine their attitude and their level of enthusiasm or opposition.

So after competence and trust, point of view is paramount. It is as though the leader is captain of the ship, looking out from the bridge to the horizon in back and the one in front. The captain can see the weather, the waves, the sharks, any land ahead, and any dangers or good omens. Most others will have a limited view, perhaps from the lower deck, and then only from a small porthole. From that point of view, it is hard to tell whether a change of course is needed or disastrous.

Hence, communicating context is vital. When people see this complete story as the leader sees it, they will have an understanding that the time is right for change. They might even decide that change is needed on their part. They will not yet, however, be committed to contributing to make it happen.

As you tell the story of where we've been and where we are, you are accomplishing three purposes. First, you are establishing a common understanding of events leading up to the status quo, including past occasions and circumstances, summarizing the current reality, and establishing the urgency or priority of what you are proposing—this is the historical context, a common understanding that becomes the foundation for a decision to change. Second, you are presenting a view of the issue that is broader than the self-interest of those involved in implementing that decision (including yourself) and large enough to hold the change you are advocating. This context has to do with values, culture, and meaning. You are offering constituents a chance to be a part of a change in an atmosphere that has seemed unchangeable, and something larger than themselves. Third, you are continuing to reinforce others' sense of your personal makeup and their feelings of trust in you—your personal connection to the history and meaning. In this way, you are building on your already-established competence and trustworthiness.

When you and your constituents have a common understanding of the context, change is a natural outcome. But most often, others haven't thought about the context that you have considered, that you know to be true; they need to be informed of it in order to make sense of what you are saying.

Building a Common Understanding

The importance of context is demonstrated daily. George Lakoff writes brilliantly about the "framing" of an issue.[1] But to me, a story from one of my favorite spiritual writers, the late Henri Nouwen, demonstrates the quandary and the importance of context to those who are listening, but who have no experience themselves. Nouwen was a Catholic priest, mystic, and teacher. One of his works, *The Genesee Diary,* recounts his experience during a seven-month sabbatical inside the cloister of the Trappist monastery at Genesee. For the monks, there were no newspapers, television, or other means of finding out what was going on in the world. Only the proctor (in this case, Father Marcellus) was privy to the *New York Times*.

Evening services in the monastery include the mentioning of "prayer intentions" by the monks. Nouwen reported the following occurrence:

> On one particular evening, Father Marcellus said, "Let us pray for the wife of the President of South Korea." . . . Then he realized that nobody except he had read the latest newspaper, and quickly added . . . "who was assassinated." . . . Then it probably flashed through his mind that nobody could understand why anyone would want to assassinate the wife of the President of South Korea, so he added . . . "while someone was trying to assassinate the President himself." . . . Then he realized that by now the monks wanted to know the end of the story, so he concluded his intention with the words. . . . "who safely escaped!"[2]

While most of us are not communicating to people as cloistered as monks in a monastery, everyone *is* cloistered in their own reality; the need for creating a new context remains. In the worlds of business and geopolitics, continuous instability and a plethora of media messages prevent many from knowing the real context and thereby determining the value of change. Very few people are willing to commit to change without a substantial education. As a leader, you have to inform people of the context—and then remind them, again and again. If you do not do so, your suggested change might well be seen as meaningless or nonsensical. Context answers the question, "why?" It has many facets.

Generational and Cultural Context

I was on a trip to the Far East when an aspiring Japanese MBA candidate engaged me in conversation in Japan's First Bank of Commerce. We had just heard a lecture about the changing relationship between Japanese banks and their customers. The young man explained to me that for the last fifty years, Japanese banks and their commercial business customers were partners with the Japanese government. The incentives for industry and financial service entities had been clearly the same over that period. Regulations, however, were now changing to give banks and the commercial customers they serve some different motivations. Accordingly, customers were no longer willing to accept the judgment of the bank without question. For the first time, the bank was being asked by customers to justify currency trades made on their behalf that turned out badly. In the absence of common goals, customers needed to know why banks make these currency trades. To respond, the bank started a series of training classes for its customers to explain the vagaries of currency trading. It took the responsibility of articulating the context for its customers.

Later in the same conversation, the young man told me that the identical problem exists between the older generation in the bank and his own peers. "The veterans have the benefit of the old culture, and we do not. Consequently, we do not understand the reason for their actions." This contextual misunderstanding was far greater than the reasons for making certain trades. In this case, the leaders of the bank had not shared the context of the historical linkages between banks, their long-time customers, and the government. Such connections run very deep and are based on the fundamental pillars of the interconnected Japanese culture and economy, and they frequently are the primary driver in actions that are taken. Because this young man and others like him had gone to school in the West, they were unfamiliar with these roots. The context that was absent for the young man and others like him was the unspoken understandings of the past and their results in the present, a connection that was not communicated by the elders.

By explaining the *why* of currency trading to its customers, this bank assured their continued loyalty. Without the why of the Japanese business culture, the young Japanese employee will perform his duties without meaning, never developing any loyalty to the institution.

While international public ownership does dilute some company values and shift some tradition-based contextual decisions, synergism is still present between the values of the owners and the organization in companies that are privately owned. Michael Nahum is president of Microencoder, an American company wholly owned by Mitutoyo Corporation, a large private technology company near Tokyo.

Michael provided a great example of cultural context and communication from direct experience. A long-time and close supplier of Mitutoyo was to show a product at a major European trade show. Unbeknownst to the supplier, Mitutoyo had committed to begin producing a competitive product and was also scheduled to have a display at the show. Speed to market was critical—it was important to launch the product as soon as possible. Still, out of respect for their long-time supplier, the parent company refrained from showing the new product, valuing the relationship more than the market advantage. They took advantage of the contact at the show to reinforce their respect for their long-time friend and to smooth the way for a transition that would honor that bond.

The same opportunity and risks of culture differences exist between generations. Young leaders might well depend on an older generation for financing, consulting, or operations expertise, and older people might not have the benefit of a fresh approach or more global understanding. One of your jobs as leader is to provide the needed information by communicating your perspective. The same generational issues exist in nearly every culture, as Baby Boomers (people born between 1946 and 1964) all over the world begin to retire from leadership positions, and their successors try to communicate with employees or constituents who grew up not knowing the Beatles, never being without a computer or an e-mail address, and—for some—having global travel experiences before they were of legal age. Others have not had the benefits of computers—or travels—and come from a context of living longer at home, shrinking possibilities, and perhaps a limited vision of a future beyond their current jobs. Still others are not familiar with collaborative work models that span continents.

Rules of the Game

Organizations, like countries, have a culture that can simply be defined as "the way we do things around here." Such a culture is constituted as "the rules of the game"—yet another context. The world of baseball offered a solid lesson in the significance of context during one of the pastime's most famous games.

Fans get chills at the mention of a "perfect game"—a game in which the pitcher has been successful in getting every batter on the opposing team out three times in nine innings. Not one player from the other team reaches first base. A perfect game is a very rare occurrence. Only one such game has ever been pitched in the World Series of baseball. The late Stephen Gould, natural scientist and author, related the story in *The Flamingo's Smile,* and credited a *New York Times* op-ed piece of November 10, 1984:

> What could be more elusive than perfection? And what would you rather be . . . the agent or the judge? Babe Pinelli (who died at age 89 at a convalescent home near San Francisco) was the umpire in baseball's unique episode of perfection when it mattered most. October 8, 1956. A perfect game in the World Series . . . and coincidentally, Pinelli's last official game as arbiter. What a consummate swan song. Twenty-seven men to the plate, and twenty-seven men down. And, since single acts of greatness are intrinsic spurs to democracy, the agent was a competent, but otherwise undistinguished Yankee pitcher, Don Larsen.
>
> The dramatic end was all Pinelli's, and controversial ever since. Dale Mitchell, pinch hitting for Sal Maglie, was the twenty-seventh batter. With a count of 1 ball and 2 strikes, Larsen delivered one high and outside . . . close, but surely not, by its technical definition, a strike. Mitchell let the pitch go by, but Pinelli didn't hesitate. Up went the right arm for called strike three. Out went Yogi Berra from behind the plate, nearly tackling Larsen in a frontal jump of joy. "Outside by a foot," groused Mitchell later. He exaggerated . . . for it was outside by only a few inches . . . but he was right.
>
> Babe Pinelli, however, was more right. A batter may not take a close pitch with so much on the line. Context matters. Truth is a circumstance, not a spot.
>
> Truth is inflexible. Truth is inviolable. By long and recognized custom, by any concept of justice, Dale Mitchell had to swing at anything close. It was a strike . . . a strike high and outside. Babe Pinelli, umpiring his last game, ended with his finest, his most perceptive, his most truthful moment. Babe Pinelli, arbiter of history, walked into the locker room and cried.[3]

Babe Pinelli was able to break the objective written rules of a national pastime by virtue of the universally understood rules—the *context* of the game of baseball and the circumstances of this particular game. Had the game been played at midseason, with nothing on the line, he would have called the pitch a ball. Or, had he called a strike, there would have been cries of "we were robbed!" In *this* case, in *this* context, the leader stated the truth, and the change was agreed to instantly by everyone in the park, everyone who was glued to a radio, and I would bet, even by Dale Mitchell.

This application of the principle to baseball is American, but the application to business and politics is global. The idea of shared context is easy to see among baseball fans, even easier among citizens of the United States; it is more challenging when applying the principle to the citizens of the world. Different cultures have different standards regarding compensation, cronyism and favors, bureaucracy, family, and ethics. While we may not compromise our own standards or rules, knowing others' is essential for global impact. Empathy assumes its highest purpose in such circumstances.

Context Has Personal Meaning

In preparing a Leadership Communication Guide, you have to consider the historical background, the deep cultural roots of the issue and the organization, and the oft-unspoken rules of the game. But you must also think through the broad implications of change and reflect on the moral consequences as you perceive them. Your constituents have not looked at the issue so thoroughly; they have not traced the issue to its conclusion, nor have they imagined themselves personally in a new future. Like the young Japanese student, they do not have the benefit of seeing this issue against the background of the "old culture." You, on the other hand, do.

Peter Senge, in researching *The Fifth Discipline,* found that a profound sense of scale was common to inspirational leaders. "Each [leader]," says Senge, "perceived a deep story and sense of purpose that lay behind his vision, what we have come to call the *purpose story*—a larger 'pattern of becoming' that gives unique meaning to his personal aspirations and his hopes for their organization . . . "[4] While this language might seem ethereal, Senge suggests that reflection on your own personal values will yield a broader and more personal context for your role as leader. Communicating this larger "purpose story" invites an audience to become a part of something larger than themselves, giving them a chance to make a difference in a bigger arena than they have perceived possible. You are giving others the opportunity to trade their commitment for greatness. Nearly all consider this a very good bargain.

Consider the fact that Nobel Laureate Stephen Hawking's first book, *A Brief History of Time,* has sold more than ten million copies in thirty languages since its publication in 1989, and was on the London *Sunday Times* best-seller list for more than four years. This is somewhat astounding, when you consider that according to the author, to read and understand this book (an explanation of the search for a unifying theory for the origin and working of the universe) would qualify the reader to start a Ph.D. in theoretical physics. Many explanations have been offered for the book's unanticipated popularity. Hawking, however, thinks the reason is simply that the general public wants to be involved in the discussion of "really big questions."

I agree. Many leaders—in all fields, particularly politics—are too quick to patronize their public, assuming that they are either selfish, dull, or uninterested in global or universal questions. Quite the contrary: the public is eager to hear, eager to engage, and eager to act when called to contribute to just causes that are larger than themselves, even when they don't understand the details. All monumental changes that eventually occur originally seem to be too great, too challenging, too costly. Just in the last twenty-five years, the destruction of the Berlin Wall, the reunification of Germany, the end of apartheid in South Africa, the beginning of nuclear disarmament, the Arab Spring—all changes seemed beyond reach. Yet each one was preceded by a call, and then by ordinary people sharing the vision and knowing the context of that call. The confidence of today's public can only be strengthened by leaders who can present change as a chance for others to have an impact on a scale that is much larger than the immediate and mundane. As the interconnectedness of the world becomes more obvious, the scale of impact simply must become larger. This is a major challenge of our time. Few leaders have the perspective to make this shift.

Where Did I Come In?

Finally, the context section of the Guide also affords opportunities to reinforce the competence and trust that you have established earlier. As Dov Seidman said in *How,* his 2007 bestseller, "In a world of constant, radical change, we all need a bulwark that will act simultaneously as propellant and guide. We need to root ourselves in what we know should never change—our values. That's why now more than ever we need people . . . rooted in sustainable values."[5] As Seidman suggests, perhaps the most important factor in the history of the issue is that your personal values have been supported or challenged by it. In the final analysis, it is your conviction about the change that's needed, supported by your values that will move others to act.

Thomas Jefferson lived in the context of "when in the course of human events." He felt the oppression of the British through, personally experiencing the frustration of taxes that he paid without representation. So it was with Ghandi, Barbara Jordan, Martin Luther King, Nelson Mandela, and Joan of Arc. Because they lived in the circumstances, they rarely had to speak of them, but it was clear that they were affected by the history of the issue, and the common knowledge of that fact made their motivations clearer, their competence more obvious.

So it is with you. While the change you are advocating might seem less significant than the changes led by these icons, the principles of inspiration are the same. Letting others know your historical experience with the issue that you are advocating—where you came in—might not strengthen the logical case for the mind, but it will compel the heart to listen as well. The mind makes a decision based on agreement with the information the speaker provides. The heart makes the commitment based on a feeling of connection to the leader. The mind looks for evidence, the heart looks for passion. The mind weighs facts, the heart acts on faith. The mind looks for purpose, the heart seeks meaning. The mind believes, the heart trusts. Both are necessary for committed action.

Creating a common understanding, providing a broader view of the opportunity, and reinforcing trust and competence—these are the purposes of communicating context. This chapter presents a few examples.

Historical Context

- What is the history of this issue? Where have we been?
- What stages have we gone through and what conditions brought them about?
- What is the story that captures the history?
- What has changed to make this issue timely and critical?
- In light of history why do we need this change now?
- Where do we currently stand?
- What role did I play in this history?

In 2011, I was fortunate to begin working with the president and general manager of the Chemical Analysis Group of Agilent Technologies. The world's best measurements company, Agilent is not only financially successful, it has developed and nurtured a culture of innovation and collaboration. Mike McMullen became general manager of CAG after an assignment in finance in Japan. He had also been active in China and Korea before accepting the job back in the United States. A Wharton MBA with a great track record, Mike was eager to actually lead something, so when he returned to the States to begin his tenure as a general manager, he was a bit dismayed to find an apparent atmosphere of gloom. The business unit had been holding its own, but people seemed to think it was on a holding trajectory.

Mike approached his new assignment as a turnaround. He was convinced that the business could not only thrive as it was, but that it also had a future that could include growth in both revenue and profitability. After a few years of executing on a refocused strategy and re-energizing the team, he was able to convince the CEO and the board to make the biggest investment in the history of Agilent—the procurement and assimilation of Varian Associates, active in the same general fields but offering synergies in both product line and geography. I was brought in the first time when the acquisition was being put together. As with most such international mergers, it became far more complicated than Mike or anyone else had anticipated, and involved some divestiture and adjustment to make all the international regulatory bodies happy.

Finally ready to exploit the advantages of the acquisition, Mike started to communicate with everyone in the organization including the board about his plans for the future. In working together on his Guide, we defined the purpose of his efforts as follows:

1. To redefine and recast the mission of CAG to allow us to take advantage of the growing opportunities in the global markets we serve—opportunities that have significant implications for some of the important issues of the world's future. Doing so will allow us to obtain investments and allocate resources to new applications in our current markets and pursue other markets appropriate in food, health care, the environment, and energy.
2. To energize others (board, family, employees of Agilent, and other stakeholders) regarding our future.
3. To frame the issues and the opportunities.

For most of the employees to understand the need for this change would require an immense context. Not all of it would be relevant to every communication, but in constructing the Guide, we included it all. After defining his own competence and establishing his trustworthiness, we began to frame the historical context. Mike chose to do this in four phases, Assessment, Engagement, Start Rolling, and Growth. Assessment was the period when he first arrived and was characterized by language like this:

> When I arrived for my first day in office, my first reaction was that we were in need of some good news. The morale was not great and when I went on the road to meet with the field it was the same; eager but a little demoralized from the lack of recent progress. From Asia, I had not fully understood what had been happening to what had once been a "crown jewel" business for the company. . . . The articulated strategy was "defend and protect," and while perhaps appropriate as a strategy, it was not an inspiring message.

Mike continued into the Engagement phase, reflected in his Guide this way:

> I knew that I had to build a new strategic plan, even though other GMs had just completed one. What was different with mine was the theory of construction. It's not just about what's in the business plan, but who contributed. I alluded earlier to a belief in true collaboration. We needed to involve the broader organization, particularly the field. Broader engagement gives you a better plan (more perspective) and the real payoff is in the delivery of the results. We built the plan on inspiration for what we could do together, and on making some very focused bets.

For the Start Rolling phase Mike recalled and documented a story:

> I was in Santa Clara reviewing the only project that we had going, when the project manager stopped me in a hall and told me that the machine under development could only do 80 percent of the applications, and would actually hurt the market. It took a lot of engagement for them to do that. I said, "OK, but I need something." They took the rest of the funds and produced, in six months, a machine that eventually gulped up the space we were looking at. It was the first sign of real life in the entire group.

Finally, Mike wrote about taking CAG into the Growth phase and spelled out what was becoming the current reality:

> Despite signs of life, every time I would go on the road, I would hear things like "You are a finance guy. You are just dressing us up to sell us." But we fixed the issues and people in the field began to believe. My boss began to see potential. Finally in 2008, we became a fully aligned business group and questions about our track record were put to rest. We got a new name and a new logo, and launched an effort to fill product and geographic holes in our business. The result was what was then the largest acquisition in the history of Agilent. We bought Varian for $1.5 billion and launched a successful integration that today has us exceeding our objectives in customer satisfaction and meeting or exceeding all of our financial targets.

Throughout the process, Mike was able to create shared historical context by cutting history into discrete pieces spanning the early years when enthusiasm was really lacking through to the integration of the company's largest acquisition.

To communicate change effectively, everyone has to share the story. Mike's Guide allows him to deliver some or all of this story when he needs to. Speaking to new employees or while recruiting, he might well relay all of it. Or a specific question could prompt him to use only a part of it, perhaps the part that related to the specific product line or country.

These excerpts illustrate that Mike has covered the history, priority, and current reality, and that we know where he came in. Yet what I've presented here is only about a quarter of the context material. His complete Guide includes much more detail, all aimed at answering the questions that began this section. And it will continue to evolve and grow in fresh iterations over the years.

The Leadership Communication Guide to change the U.S. education system begins its historical context at the turn of the twentieth century and proceeds through four phases to the current reality.

Sample from the Education Guide

Historical Context: The public education system in the U.S. really began at the turn of the twentieth century, when we were an agrarian society. Kids were needed to bring crops in during the summer, they were needed to work on the farms, and our schedule of classes was dictated by nature's schedule as much as anything else. In addition, our heritage of Christianity dictated a bit of the calendar. We set the system up to have three months off in the summer, and weekends off to work and worship. At this point, public education was not mandatory.

At the end of World War II, America had become largely industrialized. The system's objectives changed to include a robust university system and a commitment to educate

(*Continued*)

everyone. As a matter of national pride and priority, a basic education became part of the law of the land. Truancy became an enforceable concept, and the neighborhood school became a hub of a country that was quickly becoming largely suburban. Teaching was an honorable and respected profession, and the pay, if not at the top of the range, was adequate and esteeming. Women largely filled these ranks, perhaps for the wrong reason—because there were few other opportunities for them. But the result was a strong system of education . . . women were magnificent in those roles as they would later be in others. The teaching profession was able to garner the best of these women . . . bright, dedicated, and passionate about what they did.

The next significant shift came in the '60s, when we felt an urgent requirement to encourage technical education. The space race was on. . . . As our own Vanguard satellite lay beeping on the ground while the Russian Sputnik raced across the night sky, the shift to intellectual elitism was almost immediate. The "gifted" students were put on a fast track in a system meant to give fair education to all.

This is where I came in. I spent my entire high school career with the same eighteen kids, taking every advanced placement and honors course offered in math and science as well as the humanities. We were to be the next wave of American engineers. While I didn't know it, at the same time, teachers took up sides, few wanting to teach the "dumb" or "average" kids; and a combination of that argument and the recession of the early part of the decade created a resurgence in the American Federation of Teachers, swelling its ranks from 60,000 to 200,000. While the AFT did much to bolster the desegregation movement, it thrived on the membership of the average, because gifted teachers didn't need it, but others did.

Gifted students and gifted teachers have continued to leave the public schools ever since; and the stresses of the union have created an atmosphere where funding is next to impossible to gain from the populace. In general, today's inner-city public schools are underfunded, many teachers are underpaid for lack of budget, and genuinely passionate teachers have found other avenues to express their talents.

The best women, of course, now have many other opportunities, as do dedicated men who chose teaching out of their commitment to contribute. In 2007, my best student in the MBA program at the University of California was a former award-winning special education teacher. He left teaching at $30,000 per year and invested $50,000 in an MBA. His starting salary at a consulting company in San Francisco was $130,000.

Can we blame him? Of course not.

This Guide too, recognizes the history, priority, and my own personal involvement in the issue.

Broader Perspective and Meaning

- What greater purpose will be served by this change?
- What is the broadest possible implication of the current situation?
- What greater system has been harmed because of the current reality?

When Mike McMullen first looked at his new business unit, he saw immediate problems to solve. Morale was not great; people generally believed this business group was going to be flat at best. Some clients were disappointed in the performance and responsiveness of the group. All these problems had to be fixed, of course, but Mike also knew that while people will work for money, they will give their lives for meaning. He began to position his group as serving the markets that would have the longest-lasting and strongest meaning to humankind, and began to communicate through that prism. This is how he spelled out the broader reality in his Guide:

> There are two primary truths about our current position. First we are active in the most exciting set of markets on the globe. They touch literally billions of lives—energy, the environment,

> medicine, food and technology manufacturing. Everyone on the planet stands to benefit from our work.
>
> Second, we are integral to the whole of Agilent. We are part of a larger picture, in the world and in our company, and everything we do counts. Most people have heard of the DDT case from the 1950s. It was so complicated and unlikely that it took years to unravel, but it was technology like ours that allowed the issue to be solved. There was no reason to suspect that small concentrations of DDT would cause the death of scores of birds, and indeed threaten to wipe them out. Through measurement equipment like ours, it was discovered that in one Long Island estuary, concentrations of less than a tenth of a part per million of DDT in aquatic plants resulted in 3–25 PPM in gulls, terns, cormorants, mergansers, herons and ospreys—what was then a totally unpredictable result.
>
> We are engaged in discovering new versions of this very same issue. For example, we are collaborating with the University of Colorado to measure the extent to which personal care products remain in the water supply, and how their concentrations affect the health of animals and humans. What contaminants in our water and food are responsible for the ills of the world? We don't know, but we are about finding out. And we're doing it as part of a great company totally aligned to the purpose.

As a second example, it's useful to look at the way the education Communication Guide sums up the broader implications of reform.

Sample from the Education Guide

Broader Implications: This is a serious political and social problem. Why? Because at the bottom line, good education is a social vaccine that cures other serious problems. It can immunize children from pregnancy, ward off a future that might include alcohol and drug use, and make it possible for adults to inspire learning and real human growth in their posterity. It can also provide our nation with educated citizens who can vote intelligently. A democracy can only work if it is inhabited by people who participate, and who have the tools to grasp the complexities of today's world.

Educated people are productive . . . they work and contribute to society. Education is fundamental, and it should be our highest priority . . . but we have to attract talent to make it work.

Context well done includes history, priority, personal involvement, and broad implications. It reinforces the story, supports the competence of the leader, and offers a cause that is greater than the self.

Here is one more example to consider and put to the test. Although this address happened in the mid-1990s, the subject matter is relevant today, as are the elements of the structure. John Adams, then chairman and CEO of Texas Commerce Bank, was a powerful advocate for corporate adoption of practices that supported families, particularly working mothers. He delivered a speech to the National Council of Jewish Women in 1993 and later published it as a way of spreading his message. After stating the purpose, Adams continued by asking the contextual question explicitly:

> Why are corporate leaders more and more addressing work-family issues in their business planning and management?
>
> One obvious reason is the changing family. When the drive to American industrial dominance began to build steam in the 50s, the country was comfortable with the notion of a working husband and a wife at home with kids. It made sense in the wake of World War II. The men had come home. Rosie the Riveter could leave the factory. They both wanted children, and American prosperity enabled single-earner families to lead comfortable lives.
>
> Today, we must deal with new realities. Remember the guy who wouldn't dream of his wife working? He's the same guy

> who now wakes her up in the middle of the night to suggest that she ask her boss for a raise.
>
> Fewer than 22 percent of married-couple households consists of a male breadwinner and female homemaker. In the 1950s, the figure was 80 percent. Fifty-eight percent of mothers with children under six now hold paying jobs. The figure was 20 percent in 1960. And 68 percent of mothers with children under 18 work outside the home.
>
> Today, the majority of families rely on two incomes to maintain a middle class standard of living, and a significant number of families need two incomes just to pull themselves above the poverty line. Two working parents, and single parents, bring an array of needs with them into the workforce that didn't exist before.[6]

How does this speech stack up against the criteria for shared context? Certainly, the historical context is well done. There is no question that this particular group (the National Council of Jewish Women) would have a firm grasp on the history of the issue. Adams has told them "where we have been" and "where we are," and has let them know why we need to break the established rules of work.

In addition, Adams has broadened the issue to one of values that are greater than anyone's individual agenda. This change is clearly the "right thing to do" in light of the rights of women, the newer definition of the family, and the relationship of corporations to their employees.

Has he reinforced his own personal competence and trustworthiness? Do we know where he came in? Has he established himself as a leader rather than a mere carrier of information?

Not really. We know nothing about his own personal involvement in this context. We do know that he was a middle-aged man at the time, and as such, he might well have had parents who lived during World War II. His mother might well have been a "Rosie the Riveter" who came home from the factory when his father returned from overseas. His own children might well be in the current generation, coupled with mates who work in commerce and try to balance their families with their other obligations. In fact, it might well have been his daughter who got the suggestion to ask her boss for a raise. We simply don't know. As he developed this message, which resulted in this same speech being given in several venues, he could have considered adding such details, which would convert a mere set of facts to a personal reflection on those facts, and thereby raised his stature to a leader, rather than a mere presenter of data.

Evidence: Logic and Data

Cognitive evidence to support a given point of view is abundant, and leaders no longer have privileged access to that evidence. Clearly, the amount of information to be known is accelerating at a rate substantially faster than anyone's ability to know it, and accessing that information is becoming easier. The world's public, even in the most remote regions, has a wealth of data available. For that same reason, data doesn't have the power to sway people like we once believed. This is leadership communication, not staff work, so the use of data, while necessary, is not the lever you are looking for. You are going for inspiration, so values and experience are more important for your purposes as a leader.

I was trekking and traveling in the country of Bhutan for more than a month in 2001. This idyllic nation, protected by the Himalayas and its strategic position, remains a bastion of Tibetan Buddhism. At that time, the political power was shared by a king and the head of the body of monks. Citizens wear the national dress; Bhutan's countryside is streaked with flowing rivers teeming with trout that even Montanans would envy. Bhutan's perennial forests range as high as fourteen thousand feet, and rhododendrons grow to more than twenty feet tall, decorating the green conifer groves. Each village is self-contained, and life seems as though it takes place in Shangri-La. Bhutan's representative gave a speech to the United Nations in 1998 declaring that the country was actually measuring "Gross National Happiness," rather than GDP.

Yet even in this last stronghold of a nature-based culture, the Internet and CNN have invaded. Despite the plurality of opinion that the culture should eschew information technology, Bhutan is about to become "twice born." In every guest house and hotel, Indian video is the entertainment of choice. Internet cafés dot Thimpu, its capital, and even appear in its minor villages. Now, ten years after my own visit, Bhutan sports several five-star hotels. The march of information, available to nearly everyone, moves on. While we may not agree that all this information is accurate, its availability gives everyone a new reference point to measure the competence of anyone who advocates change.

I'm not sure it is for the better. To see a young Bhutanese in an Internet café rather than participating in a traditional archery contest is bittersweet, and to witness the rise in crime and erosion of ritual is dismaying, even as it is inevitable. Yet their king, like us, tries to maintain his focus on values and the social fabric of his country—he tries to make *meaningful* progress, not just progress.

As you build your Guide to inspire yourself and others, you will obviously do the research. The evidence you use and the way in which you use it are both vital to maintaining credibility. Appendix A presents a more complete discussion of the rules of evidence in leadership communication: that specifics encourage engagement, that relevance to others is critical to evidence being given weight, and that quotations from experts can be distracting or attracting, depending on how well such experts are known to you and to others. Ultimately, data, examples, and the voices of other authorities serve as excellent evidence for the mind. They help fulfill the first requirement for context: to create a common understanding of the circumstances that led up to the current situation. Expansion of the meaning of change and the bond of competence and trustworthiness are both generated by your own personal involvement with the context and your own experience with the evidence that you present.

Revealing the Personal: Showing the Passion

Once you and others have agreed on a context, you have also agreed on the need for change. You have mutually defined the width and depth of the chasm from the present to the future. To jump this chasm with you, others must be convinced of your competence and satisfied that you are trustworthy. In contrast to your competence, however, your trustworthiness is subjective. It will be established in the personal experiences, analogy, metaphors, and stories that you use to support your own authenticity.

I frequently visit Singapore on business, and on a day off, I often find myself near the waterfront in a downtown bank plaza. Standing before me is a fifteen-foot Salvadore Dali bronze, "Homage to Newton," an abstract figure of a human featuring large holes in the skull and chest. A bronze heart is suspended from fine wire in the center of the body and a brain is carved to appear suspended in the skull. The explanatory plaque indicates that it is by expressing both mind and heart that all of human enterprise is accomplished. This is, indeed, the challenge of today's leaders. Inspiring committed action requires the leader to appeal to both the heart and the mind.

We don't often do it well. To many potential leaders, particularly those trained as lawyers or business professionals, the context of a change message is where one proves the case. Particularly in Western culture, the proof is considered sacrosanct, and when others ignore this proof they are considered either incapable of grasping the truth or irresponsible. Yet each day, we see juries making decisions that seem to be totally unjustified by the facts of the case. The jurors have looked for holes in the judge's instructions that will allow them to return a verdict consistent with the direction their collective hearts lead them. To ignore this phenomenon, to disregard our ability and desire to enlarge our experience of life to include the facts and move beyond them, is to fail to lead. The jury is merely the most obvious case of proof not necessarily dictating action. Certainly there are others. Very logical public policy decisions fail in implementation because the people at the grass roots see more than reason in the faces of those they help. In other instances, decisions by corporate executives, steeped in logic, don't get carried out at the operational level.

Is it cynicism? Apathy? Inertia? Or are people just taking action despite the logic of the situation? Whatever the motivation, people are acknowledging new ways of deciding and taking appropriate action. We are not willing to merely connect all the logical digital dots to form the picture; we want to draw outside the lines of the strategic mind, to acknowledge the analog, flowing nature of life in a way that helps us live appropriately. This may not be in the cultural norms—but it is very human.

Blaise Pascal, a seventeenth-century mathematician, had a running argument with René Descartes about the axiom Descartes favored, "I think, therefore I am." The conflict was often bitter, but when Pascal became ill, Descartes attended him as a physician and stayed with him for long periods of time. When Pascal asked about his reasoning for staying with and caring for such a long-time rival, Descartes replied, "The heart has reasons that reason knows nothing of."[7]

The Context Complete

Chapter Five reviewed the purpose statement in a Guide about end-of-life decisions that Rebekah Saul Butler developed as a master's candidate at Berkeley. Her interest was in encouraging families to have discussions about death and dying before the event, to make sure that the emotional and economic realities are clear. Rebekah was concerned—on both the personal and the national level—about a meaningful process of death, and about the implications of long-term care on national policy and economics. This is a tough issue to lead; so to begin, she documented her own personal context, revealing the source of her passion:

> When I was a young girl, my grandfather grew ill with heart disease. Lucky for us, he was saved by bypass surgery. He then survived 11 great years, living very well, enjoying his grandchildren and his retirement. Over time he grew sick again with heart disease and with Parkinson's. His quality of life was poor and he was in pain. He almost died one weekend and the family flew in, pressed his suit, and wrote his obituary, when my grandfather's doctor decided to try one more heart medication and my grandfather responded. He lived two more terrible years, in a nursing home, strapped to his bed because he wanted to go home so badly he would try to crawl out of the window at night, and because his Parkinson's medication made him hallucinate and he was often frightened. When he finally died, we were relieved, because of the *awfulness* of the two years, years that my grandfather really did not want to be in this world anymore. Now when I think of my grandfather and his final years, I think of that window in his nursing home room. As a family, we were unprepared to face the end of my grandfather's life.

Rebekah clearly had some experience here. As she wrote the following broad historical context, she included logical evidence:

> At the heart of this public policy discussion was the fact that our nation is growing older. People are living longer. In 1900, life expectancy in the U.S. was 47 years. Now it's on average 77 years. In 2030, there will be over one million centenarians in the United States. No wonder we are wondering how will we best take care of our elderly.
>
> Medicare was enacted in the 1960s as a major step toward a national contract to care for older Americans. At first the program was relatively small. In the course of our lifetimes, however, it has grown and evolved to represent one of the federal government's largest expenditures . . . currently over $200 billion annually.
>
> Because there are more of us, and because we are spending more on each person, these expenditures are growing, and are expected to escalate to 10% of our GDP by 2070. They are currently just over 2%. Imagine, when we are old, one in ten dollars of our entire GDP will be spent to keep us alive.
>
> Eugene Steuerle is a senior fellow at the Urban Institute, a Washington, D.C.–based think tank. He is an economist who has spent his life studying, writing about and trying to solve social issues and fiscal problems . . . both as an academic and as an executive in the Treasury Department. In a testimony before a Senate committee considering the fiscal implication of an aging population, Dr. Steuerle put forth the following:
>
> "Every once in a while I wake up from a dream where a researcher from the NIH comes running into a hearing and proclaims, "Eureka, I've found a cure for cancer." Rather than celebrating and jumping up and down with glee, the members of the committee instead beat their brows and begin to commiserate among themselves. "What is going on here? What is their problem," I ask myself. Then suddenly I realize that they can see only the effect of the new medical miracle on the budget: higher health care costs and higher Social Security costs associated with longer lives."
>
> Indeed, it is a good dilemma that we have, but it is a dilemma.[8]

This context has it all. We know the history of the issue from the standpoint of someone who has a competent association with the problem. We have numbers, we have an authority, we know the greater meaning of the issue, and we have the personal motivation of our leader. It would be easy to get committed to this issue, and easy to follow such a competent and personally engaged person.

***

Presenting logical support for change is an essential part of leadership communication. We respect leaders who have the facts in hand, but those who rely only on mental evidence to support their positions are often judged to be uncaring technocrats. Conversely, those who rely solely on emotional appeal and conviction are considered "more real." Both these judgments are inaccurate. We are all blessed with the ability to reason and the capacity to feel, and it is the integration of these two faculties that is authentic. Leaders who can communicate both logic and passion are deploying themselves fully. Establishing a shared context is the core of a leadership message for change. Compose it well, and you will be prepared to communicate effectively and completely.

Questions to Ask in Creating Shared Context

- Common Understanding of History
  - What is the history of this issue? Where have we been?
  - What stages have we gone through and what conditions brought them about?
  - What is the story that captures the history?
- Priority
  - What has changed to make this issue timely and critical?
  - In light of history why do we need this change now?
  - Why should this be a priority in light of other important issues and priorities?
  - Is the change I am advocating the best alternative?
- Current Reality
  - Where do we currently stand?
- Reinforcement of Trust
  - What role did I play in this history?
  - Where did I come in?
- Broader View
  - What greater purpose will be served by this change?
  - What is the broadest possible implication of the current situation?
  - What greater system has been harmed because of the current reality?
  - What broader opportunities or barriers stand before us in executing this change?

Chapter Seven

Declaring and Describing the Future

The future is wonderful to contemplate, and I always consider it a miracle that we can imagine what isn't. John Schaar, a political theorist and teacher at the University of California at Santa Cruz, had this to say about our relationship to what is not yet, but could be: "The future is not some place we are going, but one we are creating. The paths are not to be found, but made, and the activity of making them changes both the maker and the destination."[1]

As a young man, I was intensely interested in the relationship between prophecy and the future. Was the prophet predicting the future or creating it? The longer I live, and the more I witness, the greater is my conviction that the prophet is the visionary who actually imagines a desirable future and then declares it to the rest of the world. In the declaration, the prophet makes something seem possible that formerly seemed impossible. In declaring the possible, the prophet moves people in the direction of making positive change. Leaders do this same work. They declare the future and they describe it in a way that is compelling to others. The third part of the Guide takes up this task.

Declaration: An Act of Creation

In the early 1980s, when the cold war was at its zenith, my business partner and I became enthralled by the application of this idea to the realm of international politics. Could leaders, imbued with enough power and imagination, begin the creation of a future that was beyond the current imagination of others, even across national and cultural lines? Could such leaders accomplish this beginning with declaration? Research seemed to suggest that not only could great shifts begin this way, but indeed they could not begin without such declaration. The Reformation, the creation of the United States, the freeing of slaves in America, the American trip to the moon—these and other great shifts in culture or accomplishments of great goals were all first conceived and then given voice by a leader.

This insight led us to some intense voluntary involvement with corporate and political leaders to suggest that the declaration of leaders could play a central role in shifting the perception of the world regarding the nuclear arms race. The available examples suggested that the greater the change that was desired, and the greater the perceived power of the leader, the more likely that the change could actually occur. The two of us were clear that if he or I declared the end of the cold war, no one would notice. What was needed was the conviction of change by leaders of the most powerful nations on earth.

Ronald Reagan and Mikhail Gorbachev stepped into this historic opportunity in 1986. When they met for a hasty summit in Reykjavik, Iceland, these two men were perceived by the world to have power over the fate of the arms race—perhaps over the fate of the earth. The Reykjavik summit was known for a time as the "do-nothing" summit. No great agreements were signed, none were reached. The end of the summit did not produce conventional rhetoric. Rather, both leaders declared that the world would never be the same. Here are their comments, quoted in the *New York Times:*

> Reagan: "Mr. Gorbachev and I got awfully close to historic agreements in the arms reduction process. We took discussions into areas where they have never been before."
>
> Gorbachev: "This was an important event. It has been a reassessment and has created a qualitatively new situation. And nobody is now in a position to act the way he was able to act before."[2]

Gorbachev's words were prophetic: "a reassessment . . . has *created.*" He did not say "a reassessment has *predicted.*" The power of these statements, the declaration by both leaders of the dawning of a new way of perceiving things, created the road to the end of the cold war. Shortly after this meeting, after years of necessary but fruitless negotiation, the details of the Intermediate Range Missile Agreement were worked out, the first missiles were destroyed, and the world quietly shifted course. The cold war came to an end in 1988, and while one could certainly argue the merits of the outcome, this change occurred almost as described in Chapter Six: "All truth passes through three stages. . . . First it is ridiculed, second it is violently opposed, third it is accepted as being self-evident."

To be recognized at all, new truth has to be declared. This starts the process from ridicule to opposition to acceptance. Sometimes these stages take decades, sometimes less, but once the seeds are planted, they indeed grow through inspiration and imagination. It is worthy to note that in 2009, the president of the United States won the Nobel Peace Prize largely based on his Prague declaration, a speech that he delivered a mere three months after being sworn in. It may well be that this speech created the possibility for the next major shift on the nuclear weapons front. "So today, I state clearly and with conviction America's commitment to seek the peace and security of a world without nuclear weapons. I'm not naive. This goal will not be reached quickly—perhaps not in my lifetime. It will take patience and persistence. But now we, too, must ignore the voices who tell us that the world cannot change."[3] Pollyanna? Perhaps. But so was the possibility of the end of the cold war, landing on the moon, creating a State of Israel, freeing the slaves in the United States, finding the "new world" in the fifteenth century. Transformation continues, and it will be up to the next generations to make it real.

While most of us don't perceive ourselves as having the power to affect the fate of the earth, each of us can imagine, each of us can—and in fact does—inspire progress in some arena, even if it is only in our own lives. We talk to ourselves incessantly, especially around turning points, large and small, personal and public. "I'm getting back to the gym," "I do," "We are family," and Chuck Schwab's public declaration—"This company will become the most useful and ethical financial services company in the world"—these are all everyday examples of the power of our psyches to imagine and declare new possibility.

The leader who is formulating and advocating change is like Oscar Wilde's visionary: "A dreamer . . . one who can find his way by moonlight, and see the dawn before the rest of the world."[4] The leader is the young Parsifal, returning from his psychic quest—a trip to his imagination—with a boon, a new dream. He has now told us that we must follow him, change our ways and put ourselves at risk in order to enjoy the future as it could be.

Walt Disney's imagination was legendary, and although he died in 1966, five years before the opening of the new Walt Disney World in Florida, he was still the instigator and the leader. It's said that at the ribbon cutting to the new park, a friend remarked to Walt's brother, Roy, "It's a shame that Walt couldn't have lived to see it." Roy's response? "Oh, Walt saw it years before we ever broke ground." Leaders simply must have this capability to see another future, and then be able to describe the dawn to those who can't see it, those who reside in the dark. What will we see when the sun comes up? What will our world look like when we have completed the change?

Making It Real: Spelling Out the Alternatives

The Leadership Communication Guide includes two elements in this section: a description of the new world that excites the leader and an equally vivid description of the world without the change. The stakes of inaction are just as important as the stakes of action. This is not the place in the Guide to dwell on the means; it calls for a focus on the eventual result of our combined effort or the consequences of doing nothing. Neither is it time to dwell on the hardship of the journey; it is a time to describe the allure of the destination. Obviously, the new future is a result of actions that we might or might not take, but the mere description of the actions themselves will not move others to act.

Antoine de Saint-Exupéry extolled the benefits of adhering to this principle: "If you want to build a ship, don't drum up the men to gather wood, divide the work and give orders. Instead, teach them to yearn for the vast and endless sea. As for the future, your task is not to foresee it, but to enable it."[5]

Chapter Three explored the power of metaphor, story, and personal experience to create and sustain culture and to inspire others to want to struggle together for a desired future state. Stories of the past and present provide evidence of need. Stories of the future provide a magnet to satisfy that need through change. To be committed, others have to see themselves in a movie-like image, playing a part in a story that is compelling, moving toward a state or objective that is more interesting and desirable than the status quo. The same is true for you.

To do this, to describe the future in a way that you and others can see and feel it, requires the courage, capability, and curiosity of the fiction writer—it is an act of imagination. Seeing and feeling yourself visually and viscerally in the changed state is a powerful draw toward moving to that state. Whether it's called *affirmation, positive thinking, prophecy, visioning,* or *strategy,* it is a way to create the future rather than to predict it.

The same futuristic and imaginative characteristic that was so prevalent in Walt Disney is present in every effective leadership communication. Listen to Henry Ford's audacious declaration, in 1903, of the future of the automobile.

> I will build a motor car for the great multitude. . . . It will be so low in price that no man making a good salary will be unable to own one . . . and enjoy with the family the blessing of hours of pleasure in God's great open spaces. . . . When I'm through, everyone will be able to afford one, and everyone will have one. The horse will disappear from the highways, the automobile will be taken for granted . . . [and we will] give a large number of men employment at good wages.[6]

Consider that this comment was made when the horse was the primary means of transport, there was very little infrastructure to support the automobile, and in fact, the motor car was thought to be only a novelty. Ford's commentary was an act of courage that inspired others to work toward the future he described. The result was not just the Ford Motor Company but a new way of manufacturing that transformed much of American industry. Steve Jobs envisioned a computer in every home, and indeed many of the first Macs were installed in kitchens to keep recipes cataloged and up-to-date. Jobs and Gates inspired, others became infected, and now we are off to new electronic horizons. Can we wonder if those early declarations about the cold war, about nuclear arms, about space travel, will be infectious enough, will be the subject of other leaders, in a way that in one more generation we are marveling at their efficacy? Will we see the same in energy and education? As a species, there is no doubt that we have the potential inside of us to make all of it real.

Certainly we know that in principle, if you can't envision a future that is compelling, you can't lead. You simply won't know where you are going. Putting in the work on their Leadership Communication Guides has helped many leaders envision the future.

Describing the Future

- What new reality will be created with the change?
- How will we personally be affected by the change?
- What rich description (image) can I provide for what it will look like when we have completed the change?
- What value will be affirmed by the change?

When Mike McMullen and I first met, he was already the epitome of a business manager. As he began to develop the Communication Guide that would inform his presentations to the board, company, analysts, and others about the future of the Chemical Analysis Group, he realized that he had been reluctant to talk about anything that was not real—meaning anything that wasn't producing revenue today. For certain financial groups, that is an appropriate approach; but even with these constituents, it might still be appropriate to share your imagination, particularly if you make it clear that you are not predicting but imagining. As Mike and I worked together on developing his Guide, he was particularly taken by the prospect of moving measurement devices into the field and porting them to smaller and smaller receptors. In developing countries this is a particularly important idea, since they do not have the infrastructure in place to support large-scale laboratories. As we were discussing this reality, Mike described one particular device that measures the characteristics of material for major new aircraft. The device is portable, hand-held, about the size of an iPad, and is carried from plane to plane to measure certain parameters of material. It is battery-powered and light in weight, yet very precise.

We began to dream about what portability might mean in the future, and eventually he wrote the following:

> We are engaged in four of the most exciting and dynamic areas of the world's future:
>
> - Safe and adequate food and water supplies and their distribution to where they are needed most.
> - The discovery and delivery of new sources of energy.
> - Monitoring and protection of the environment.
> - More precise and efficient materials design and fabrication.
>
> I have to start this part of the effort by admitting that it is hard for me to talk much about efforts that are not currently in a real pipeline to produce revenue. That's probably because I'm so results oriented. But when I survey the possibilities for CAG, I get excited, and I'd like to share some of that excitement with you in this portion.
>
> It is our aim to make the people of the world healthier and safer. Just a few examples and a few dreams:
>
> In the environment, food and water . . . one such opportunity is in *Mobile Measurement,* a movement that is growing around the world. The idea suggests that we can test samples at the source rather than having to take samples back to a central laboratory. Developed countries have "sunken funds" in wired infrastructure, but in China, India, Brazil, and Russia . . . and yes, even Africa, wireless is the standard. They will not have to dig ditches and run cable and wire, and they won't have to sink a large investment into underground infrastructure for their information systems. The same could be said for laboratories. As we miniaturize and put more function in the actual hands of analysts, centralized labs will become less necessary, and the trade-off will be instant results right in the field. A portable ultrasound device that is run by an iPhone is

> already expanding the capabilities of doctors in remote parts of Africa.
>
> We have developed a mobile lab in China with new Agilent instrumentation that allows our clients to bypass the need to develop a laboratory infrastructure, including sample collection and transport, and are bringing the ability to analyze close to the sample for immediate determination of any health hazard due to a spill or other incident. We can also do routine monitoring of discharge in the water system by farmers and industry for pollution detection and ultimately improve the safety of the water supply. We can help pharmaceutical companies and government officials quickly identify counterfeit drugs. This is a huge issue in developing parts of the world like Africa . . . where a desperately needed drug often does not provide help because doctors are unknowingly giving counterfeit medication to the children in need.
>
> And if you really want to dream, consider a future where citizens will be empowered and equipped to do real-time environmental testing wherever they are, transmit the readings and display them on a GPS-based map for their community, their government, or the world to see. The device could easily be a cell phone, with an application to test the air. Sensors would convert the analog sample to digital and display the air quality of their area on a revolving graphic of the earth. Imagine over a billion people testing the air in that way, and everyone having access to the result. This is only one possibility. We could do the same with water, food, or soil, and of course, we could use the same ideas in areas where there are known contaminants, like nuclear power sites.

Will Mike say it this way every time? Of course not. But the reflection on the future and the writing of the imaginary conditions will allow him to communicate with others in a way that can be compelling. More important, it gives him a clear target, a sensory-rich set of thoughts and feelings that will keep him inspired and keep him communicating about the possibilities in the change that he is advocating. Mike has plenty of juice in this Guide to inspire him, and therefore others. He has sketched a new reality that is vivid, exciting, and absolutely possible.

In advocating the need to be more direct about end-of-life discussions, Rebekah Saul Butler envisioned a future entirely different from the actual reality of the past. Had her family invoked the change in attitude and action about end of life conversation that she was advocating for others, it would have looked like this:

> When I imagine the future, I think of how things would have been different in my own family had we had these conversations before my grandfather grew ill. Some summer, during my family's annual visit to Texas, we would have been sitting around the living room after dinner, the smell of pot roast and cornbread still lingering, and someone . . . maybe my grandmother, would bring it up: "We're getting older, you know," my grandmother would venture. "It's about time for us to start thinking about our futures." We would talk about their financial security, housing options, retirement communities. And we would talk about decision-making protocols around health care treatment; seeing a lawyer to put in place some legal mechanisms, like Advance Directives, maybe a do-not-resuscitate order. In the course of the conversation, my grandfather might say, "I don't care what happens, I don't want to live in a nursing home. If I get really sick, let my time come." My grandmother might have a different perspective. Maybe she would want us to choose to do everything possible to keep her alive; she fears death, wants to postpone it.
>
> Then, several years later, in the hospital, the cardiologist would tell us, "Your grandfather is not going to make it on his current treatment. I can change his medication, but I want you to know, he will never regain his health; he will be debilitated, and his Parkinson's symptoms will grow worse." We would then approach my grandfather, ask him what he wants, go over the options, remind him that he once made us promise he wouldn't end up in a nursing home, perhaps review his living will. I don't think that this final conversation will ever be easy, but it will be easier, and more fruitful, if we have conversations earlier in life as well.

This kind of personal vision is especially effective, as it gives us the direct impact of the change on our own lives. Reflecting on your own experience of how it could have been different for you is a particularly effective way of thinking about it—and a particularly effective way of communicating the benefits to others. Most of us can see ourselves in Rebekah's future, either having the conversation with our parents or having the conversation about ourselves with our own children.

Rebekah knew, from firsthand experience, the results of inaction, and she could clearly contrast that with the future she envisioned. As leaders, we need to contrast and document the differences in action and inaction for others.

The Stakes of Alternative Futures

- What are the intrinsically valuable and intangible benefits of acting on this change?
- What makes the change personally worthwhile, even though it may be painful?
- What tangible, quantitative, or hard benefits will we achieve with the change?
- How will we be affected if we don't act? Will it violate our values not to act?

Many people have difficulty envisioning the conditions that will exist if changes are made. They merely have this vague feeling that things will be better; for many people it is easier to envision what will exist if the changes are *not* made. Recording both the best case and the worst case can be as stimulating to a leader as only seeing the bright future. In fact, much of the time, it will be useful to communicate both possibilities. The next selection shows what I imagined when thinking through the alternative realities in the future of the education system.

Sample from the Education Guide

Describing the Future: Try to picture current inner-city schools converted into smaller, technology-based learning centers for both adults and children. Cooperative learning with parents would assure mutual support. Kids go to school supported to excel rather than seeing school as a prison to break into or out of. The family grows together. We can afford to put small computers into most homes, enough so that the learning could be reinforced in the evening. And picture a place in an inner-city neighborhood called a *community learning* center with flexible year-round schedules—and it doesn't sport razor wire. Rather it is protected and honored by the community itself, the parents and shopkeepers, big business and small, who regularly support the effort with their presence and their contributions. Businesses support it because these schools supply smart labor. Parents support it because they are part of it: they reap the benefits themselves in greater work possibilities and through their children who will be alive past their twentieth birthdays. Gangs begin to wilt, pregnancy rates go down as self-esteem improves from achievement. Drug dealers are no longer welcome and are slowly purged from the community. In fact, the word *community* takes on a whole new meaning. The nation, in about fifty years, reaps the benefit . . . not only from a greater and more astute workforce, but from a marked increase in people participating in their government.

There is an alternate reality, and if we don't act, we can expect it in the short term. We are already seeing the beginnings: A nation made up of only two elements, elitists and have-nots, with a growing fence around the inner city public schools, getting taller and taller, and accumulating row after row of razor wire—to keep people out, and keep the inmates in. In the meantime, those who can afford it walk around the area or move away from it, educating their young in private schools, detached from the real world of diversity, hoping to get by without getting involved. This will continue until the inevitable revolution, the violent one that always occurs when the disparity becomes more unbearable than the risk of death.

I believe that the human spirit is capable of great progress; but only if we see the issue, believe in its importance, and are willing to act.

This might well seem too dramatic or too extreme for some, but remember, it is only an example; it is an imagined consequence, both good and bad. A leader must have the ability to see and articulate both. What you use in any given communication is a choice.

In similar fashion, as an MBA student, Josie Gaillard developed the following Communication Guide to articulate her belief in the importance of U.S. independence from foreign oil supplies, envisioning and recording her alternate futures:

> If we continue to depend on foreign oil, I can promise you a future of oil shocks and recessions, poor Middle East relations and continued threats of terrorism. Families, like mine, will continue to live in fear of recession, in fear of the day OPEC members decide to raise oil prices and send our economy into a tailspin. Children will continue to wonder why those angry people on the news hate us so much. Those same children will stay awake at night wondering when the next hijacked plane is going to fly into a nuclear power plant near their homes.
>
> Now imagine a world in which the U.S. economy grows and prospers, unaffected by foreign oil prices. Imagine a world in which the U.S. is perceived as a neutral player, objective in its support of forward-looking nations and regimes while distancing itself from corrupt or repressive regimes. If we can reduce or eliminate our dependence on foreign oil by developing alternative technologies, I see a future of economic independence and greater objectivity in our foreign policy. This future will indeed bring peace and prosperity to you and me.

Creating the World We Want

These last two chapters, *Creating Shared Context* and *Declaring and Describing the Future,* detail the components of the necessary narrative for change. Without the past and future being framed and understood or imagined, those with whom we communicate will not have the necessary limbic understanding of what we want to do.

During the 2012 presidential campaign in the United States, neither candidate succeeded in communicating these key elements, context and future, with any consistency or cogency. The campaign was largely an argument about the same set of facts. Most of the rhetoric was about the weedy details of policy or was a personal attack on the opponent. None of it was connected to a past, present or future. Proposed plans and policy were presented without the support of a compelling narrative, a narrative that David Gergen, advisor to four presidents, characterizes as a clothesline. "You adopt your clothesline, and then you hang all your policies from it. (The candidates) are missing the clothesline."[7] Don Baer, former President Clinton's communication director, commented "They haven't talked about how the pieces of the puzzle fit together and move us forward from where we've been.[8]

The story needs to be told and retold, embodied by the leader and transmitted to those he wants to engage.

From the practical to the mythological, all progress is made by imagination. From new transportation to magnificent entertainment to shifts toward nonviolence to changes in energy supply, we move because someone dreams and then communicates. Josie wrote her Communication Guide as a graduate student, but as with everyone else I have presented in the examples, her writing foreshadowed her life's commitments. She became a marketing professional at a solar power company and then began her own company that promotes recyclable wrapping material. She volunteers at her church, encouraging members to do home energy audits. She and her husband are building zero-carbon energy neutral lives.

***

There are enough problems to work on. Some seem small, and others are daunting in their complexity. For each of these issues, there are many potential champions. Everyone can dream, everyone can communicate, but a select few create by speaking up and inspiring themselves and others to act. The next chapter takes up that final part of the Guide. Can we muster the conviction of a Josie Gaillard? Can we act?

Questions to Ask in Declaring and Describing the Future

- Describing the Future
  - What new reality will be created with the change?
  - How will we personally be affected by the change?
  - What rich description (image) can I provide for what it will look like when we have completed the change?
  - What will our world look like when we have completed the change?
  - What value will be affirmed by the change?
- Stakes of Alternative Futures
  - What are the intrinsically valuable and intangible benefits of acting on this change?
  - What makes the change personally worthwhile, even though painful?
  - What tangible, quantitative, or hard benefits will we achieve with the change?
  - How will we be affected if we don't act? Will it violate our values not to act?

Chapter Eight

Committing to Action

Even in ancient lore, action was recognized as the loudest voice of the committed soul. In *Monkey,* one of the most revered myths in China, emissaries of the Bodhisattva Kuan-yin retrieve the scriptures of the Greater Vehicle of Buddhism from India. On their quest, the priest's disciples often get into insult-throwing contests with demons, but one axiom is true. "The men of old said, 'What the mouth speaks proves nothing; only by deeds can men be judged.' "[1]

Leading Out Loud culminates in action. Once you have documented yourself as an emissary of the message, you will have to decide, listening to both your outside and inside calling, what you are willing to risk to see your new reality manifested. As you near completion of the development of your Guide and begin to see the possibility of a new future, you also begin to see the first steps you need to take along the path. Some are general and organizational, others are deeply personal, and still others must be taken by those you want to inspire. This chapter provides questions and gives examples to help you launch the reality that began in your imagination.

Organizational and Personal Steps Toward Change

- What steps does the organization need to take to effect the change?
- What is the strength of my personal commitment?

- What specific action am I taking personally regardless of what others may do that is significant enough to inspire them?

If you are leading a group, you will need to think through and articulate the steps that the organization, institution, company, or family needs to take to move from the status quo to the new future. This process helps you imagine the outcome, and it helps your constituents see their roles more clearly as you describe the steps.

The greater the change, the greater the need to break things down into doable steps. Consider what it took to go from imagining a man on the moon to those first actual steps on the surface of the moon. In tackling that mission, the U.S. lunar landing program was broken down into a chart of tasks that would eventually lead to the goal. The first chart was far from complete. Several of the boxes representing the early steps in the project read, "technological breakthrough needed here." Yet despite the obvious holes, thinking through the critical project benchmarks made a difference in the energy available for its accomplishment. So it is with smaller-scale change. Steps help move you and others toward an outcome, down a logical path.

The steps for the United States in moving from dependence on foreign oil might well look like what Josie Gaillard composed in her Guide:

> This is a large problem which requires a steady commitment over years; but here are the fundamental steps we have to take as a nation. First we have to convince our leaders to declare this goal of independence as a priority in a fixed time frame in order to engage the imagination of the nation. Second, we have to revise our tax policy to encourage the development of alternative energy sources. This will fuel the innovative spirit of those who have the engineering ability to find substitutes for our substantial appetite. Some of these, if not most of them, are in the oil business today. Finally, we have to begin to convert the industries and products that use the greatest amounts of fossil fuels. Automotive engines are first, industrial facilities are next, and power plants are not far behind.

Josie wrote this Guide in 2002 and, perhaps not surprisingly, the steps she articulated are just as valid today as they were then. These are the institutional action plans that will give others the guidance they need to plug their own talents into the process.

Similarly, Mike McMullen suggested a three-point agenda to stimulate conviction in CAG as a growth company:

> First: We are finishing the integration of our acquisition in order to return our overall gross profit percentages to company standards. This is a short-range issue, and will complete what we started two years ago. We are already looking at our logistics again, and we are continuously looking for more synergies in our manufacturing and supply chain. These must be a constant point of focus. Our consolidation of manufacturing and logistics with our partners in the other groups will take us a long way toward streamlining the supply chain.
>
> Second: We are growing the core. We are now solidly the number one player in most of our markets, and we have shown that we can consistently grow our base business. Having said that, we are busy in the labs and in our mergers and acquisitions group looking for ways to augment our position in our geography and in our market coverage.
>
> Third: We are driving hard in adjacent markets, both geographic and technological. We are taking advantage of our physical presence and our current technology to go beyond where we are. The world's population just went over the 7 billion mark last month, and more and more countries are facing the issues of rapid industrialization and a move from the farms to the cities. All of these countries require our products and our presence. India, China, Brazil and Russia get the most ink, but there are other places in the world only a short distance behind. In addition to geographic expansion, we have to continue to create new technology applications for our products and our minds to address. We need to develop even more partnerships with thought leaders and university research facilities to move into that future of nano-measurement, of measurement of unsuspected substances, of mobile measurement, alternative energy, and new material. This is what it will take for us to remain the leader in the

> measurement of food and water to assure a growing population of supply and safety.
>
> We have a business that deals in the most basic and most important of human problems. Our products could and should touch every person on the planet every day, even if they don't know it. We are addressing the very issues that are central to a growing planet. It doesn't get more meaningful than that.

Several months were required to articulate these three key points: further integrate the acquisition to stimulate gross profit, build the core business, and aggressively use its current strengths to expand into markets adjacent to its geographic presence and technological expertise. These three points then became Mike's mantra—the essence of his messages to every one of his constituents and a constant guide for their action.

Such statements mark the clear path for the organization and stimulate others to find their place in the plan. Once that framework is integral to the Guide, it sets the stage for you to make your own commitment to the plan, to take your own action as a way of getting movement started. It is easy to continue to plan and discuss, but ultimately, it is the leader's personal commitment to act that will inspire others to move.

Personal Commitment, Personal Action

In his meticulous study, *Authentic Leadership: Courage in Action,* Robert Terry analyzes historic definitions of leadership and concludes: "If there is one dominant connection . . . it is action."[2] The leader can observe, contemplate, study, and speak—and in fact must do all of these well. But change only happens with action. Action is what we hear about, because without it, the message means nothing.

"I can attack with three divisions in the morning." These were the words of General George Patton in 1945 when Eisenhower asked several generals how long it would take them each to be ready for an assault on Berlin. Because of this crisp and dramatic response—and his superiors' confidence in Patton's readiness—he was given the plum assignment of the campaign, the one that he believed to be the culmination of his life as a warrior.

Personal action is simple and eloquent; it sets possibility in motion, as I've learned many times in my own life.

In my late forties, I ran across the United States with eighteen other people in a transcontinental relay. The race was staged to raise awareness and money for a drug and alcohol prevention program in California. Each runner was responsible for about one and a half hours of running a day; and it was to be a race against time, not other teams. Only one other official attempt had been made to do this run, four years previously, and the record was more than sixteen days. Our team's goal was break this record for the three thousand miles from San Francisco to the steps of the Capitol in Washington, D.C.

The leader of the group was Andy Mecca, at the time the director of Drug and Alcohol Programs for the State of California. Andy is a smart and dramatic dreamer, an inspiring leader, and of course a very accomplished amateur athlete. Under his leadership, a small group of us had planned the event for a year, honing the message, raising money, recruiting our team, and arranging logistics.

We left San Francisco on September 11, 1989, at 6 a.m. I was privileged to be in the group of four with Andy, and we spent the time we weren't running in the same RV, grabbing whatever sleep we could, eating as much as possible, and moving to our next rendezvous.

The team ran night and day on Highway 50, moving across Colorado, Kansas, and into the Midwest. We crossed the Mississippi at Hannibal, Missouri, the night before a hurricane raked the southern coast of the United States, and made it into the rolling countryside of Illinois, through Indiana and Ohio. We touched West Virginia, and the day before we were due to arrive in Washington, our team ran the baton into Virginia, turned it over to the next team of four, and drove to the next rendezvous point.

We were scheduled to take the baton at 4 a.m. the same day we were to enter the District of Columbia and finish the race, but found ourselves parked and waiting on an access road for commuters into the city, a narrow two-lane road with ruts in the soft shoulders made by the eighteen-wheelers that had to move to the side to allow oncoming traffic to pass. It was raining hard and the wind was coming out of the east directly into our face. The wipers on the RV had no chance to keep up.

For the first time on the trip, it felt like the continuity of the relay was in danger. We had managed to glean great cooperation from law enforcement all the way, but to control traffic on this stretch of highway, this close to our nation's capital, was to threaten the commute of high-level public servants, an impossible hurdle to negotiate. We were stopped at a turnout waiting for the runner to approach from behind, talking to our contact in Washington—who was advising us to wait two hours until daybreak to continue.

Clearly, it was unsafe to do otherwise, but the run had not stopped for fourteen days, and we felt that stopping would also mean abandoning our chance at the record. The spirit was high, and the Navy chorus would be waiting at the Capitol along with many of the California congressional party. Pennsylvania Avenue was to be closed for us at the appropriate time.

Four of us were discussing the pros and cons as rain pelted the RV, and the wind moved the vehicle slightly from side to side as we saw the faint glow of the runner's flashlight appear in the rearview mirror, its bearer moving toward us for the exchange. In mid-discussion, Andy simply stepped out of the RV, took the baton and started his reliable stride down the shoulder of the road. We had no choice but to follow. He didn't relinquish the baton until daylight, when safety was assured. It was an elegant, inspiring, and decisive act of leadership that I will never forget. We set the record by nearly a day—fifteen days and one hour, for just over three thousand miles.

Could we have finished ahead of the old record anyway? Probably, but it would not have been a continuous run. We would have been compromised, knowing that it wasn't quite the same; and we would have wondered for the rest of our lives if we lacked the courage to reach our goal. Andy took the risk himself, and by doing so, made it possible for all of us to realize our dream of nearly two years. I'm sure in that moment before he stepped out, Andy knew that discussion would yield nothing, and that his action would galvanize the rest of us. I'm also sure that if need be, he would have run the baton all the way to the Capitol on his own.

The leader's commitment to action is the culminating and defining step of the change process. Critical as it is to know that the cause is important to you, to formulate your message so that it is clear and deep, to connect with the emotions of others, to define meaning, to create a shared context, and to describe a future that is compelling, the final difference between the leader and others is a commitment to act. It is action that signals the victory of value over habit, of meaning over safety. It is a time when we are willing to stand for what is important. This action might be in firing someone, in closing doors, in compromising compensation, in stepping out of the RV, or in going to the Knesset, but it always speaks to the leader's commitment to the absolute need for change.

Accordingly, after describing the compelling future, your Leadership Communication Guide has to reflect your personal commitment to act, and to act decisively. It is when you are developing this part of the Guide that you will discover just how important your vision is. This section of your message is the most essential to write, and when you are writing it, you should feel as though you are at a threshold, perhaps about to open a door and look out into a void of sameness. Your decision is whether to step out or remain safely static. You will hear the voices in your head discussing your shortcomings, the severity of the risk you are about to take. You will be giving yourself advice like "I need another degree," or "I don't have enough experience," or you will be hearing the voices of doubt: "I'm not senior enough in the organization," "I don't have enough savings," or "I need to take a workshop before I do this." These are all just euphemisms for "I don't like looking out that door." Just as discovering what matters, discussed in Chapter One, is an introspective process that brings forth values, the commitment to act will bring forth your fears—and ultimately, your conviction.

As you write this part of the Guide, consider the impact of the action you propose to take. Andy stepped out of the RV on a rainy, windy dark morning. He could have said, "I'll tell you what, we'll wait here for an hour or so and see what happens." He could also have said, "Let's wait and talk to the others about it." Neither of these decisions would have inspired anyone, and neither of them would have displayed the courage of his convictions.

As you think about your commitment, picture it on an "impact" meter, similar to an applause meter. At the left side, the meter says, "I'll commit to call a meeting of others to discuss this further." At the right side of the meter it says, "I'll commit to put 100 percent of my bonus on the line. If we succeed, I get all of it; if we fail, I get none of it." Perhaps on the left, the meter says, "I'll give a speech" and on the right it says, "I'll redirect my life."

This particular measurement was created by Christy Tonge, an executive coach and committed leader in her own right. She developed a passion around the gap between the "haves" and "have-nots" in Silicon Valley. She and her husband Barry are central to an organization (Reach Potential) that makes it possible for low-income kids to pursue dreams that they might not have otherwise even considered. To be fully involved, Christy and Barry left their suburban home in Mountain View and moved their family (including their two small children) to an apartment in the heart of their constituency. With other principals, they have expanded the program to include a day-to-day presence, tutoring, mentoring, and summer camps. When I first heard of her commitment, I was compelled to act as well. Christy was not just committing to raise money to provide weekly tutoring. She moved her own family, joined a community, and changed the course of her life and that of her family in order to realize the dream she had for others. The impact meter is pure Christy; she fully understands the value of action.

The difference in the two ends of the meter is obvious, and becomes even more obvious when it's not just money on the line. Consider the commitments of other leaders like Christy who changed the world on an even bigger stage. Anwar Sadat went to speak to the Israeli Knesset, and doing so cost him his life. Martin Luther King, Gandhi, and Nelson Mandela each committed to act in nonviolent opposition to the forces of oppression. They knew their message well, they delivered it well, and then they acted, with great risk of personal harm.

This principle has application in situations of far less significance.

After the Internet bubble burst in 2000, the Charles Schwab Corporation was facing severe layoffs in its ranks. The senior team met to consider their course of action. Without hesitation, the co-CEOs announced that their purpose was to keep as many people working as possible consistent with producing fair returns. They cut their own total pay by more than 90 percent for the year. Other officers followed suit, taking cuts from 50 percent to 15 percent depending on their relative position in the company. Each person took a pay cut in proportion to the opportunity they'd had to exceed their planned earnings in the boom period.

Only then did this team begin to consider what other cuts would have to be made. During the deliberations, employees volunteered to take pay cuts, to job-share, to take all of their vacations rather than accrue the compensation. They were inspired by the commitment to action shown by their leaders.

We saw few acts like this in the 2007–2009 collapse, and very little inspiration ensued. In fact, most so-called leaders in the huge financial services firms and auto companies were far more concerned with short-term gains or personal financial hardship than with the vision or values of their firms. In the end, the closest we came to inspiration was an act of Congress, not exactly the strongest emotional stimulus possible.

Other leaders I describe in the text have also made personal commitments that were inspiring. You met John Ure in Chapter Five, struggling with his supply chain and formulating a Guide to streamline the process from supplier to end user. In considering the implications of the supply chain remedy he was proposing, John made his own notes about his commitment and the cost to him personally:

> I intend to focus on our top 10 suppliers to each business unit, travel around the world and visit them and any other elements in the chain in the next 2 months where my customers, you, the business units, feel this will help, and deliver the message you and I want them to hear. This might not sound like a chore; my five-month-old son thinks it is. He prefers me to tuck him in at night, and for me, every day away from him is like a year lying naked in an igloo. I plan to kick any stone out of the path that we agree on, and clear away any

> detritus I find hidden there. I do not plan to divert from this task until I hear you cry "Enough, we do not need or indeed want you anymore!"

John made this commitment even though he could have delegated it. His courage and commitment set the stage for him to ask others to come along—and for others to want to.

When I was constructing my Leadership Guide on Education Reform, I had to consider my own time and resources. Education, to me, is *the* major social issue, and to impact it at all, one needs to be in the arena. After considering and writing and gauging my own commitment by the excitement I felt in the documentation, I was able to make this commitment, as shown in the next selection.

Sample from the Education Guide

Action: For my part, I will become a pied piper for this discussion. I speak all over the United States, mostly in business venues, and these ideas will be aired many times in the next few years as an example that others will use. I will raise enough awareness and money to find, inspire, and support an expert in the field of education to carry this banner. Within five years, we can have something on the ballot in California that will take a major step in such reform.

I have since found an institute in Singapore (National Education Institute) whose values and mission fit with my own. It has affiliates in the United States—one of them at the University of California at Santa Barbara, and I've been able to connect regarding our common vision. There is great momentum around education reform here—some controversial but most of it aimed at the same objectives. The Gates Foundation, of course, is pouring resources into the problem, but my favorites are people who are involved personally, like Christy and Barry Tonge, Michelle Rhee, Geoffrey Canada, the founders and operators of KIPP Public Charter Schools across the country, and Rebecca DeCola and the co-directors of the Lyons Community School. Dominique Lasseur and Catherine Tatge, Emmy winners and creators of Global Village Media also belong, as they spend their own resources to empower high school students to participate in the Civic Life Project, identifying local civic issues, interviewing public officials and making documentary films of their involvement. Yes, these individuals may be criticized by others, but they are courageous, and are taking direct, personal action. They are also the most likely to actually make a difference in how the issue turns out. Their action and personal commitment are eloquent.

Involving Others—Asking for Commitment

- What specific actions am I going to ask of others to give them a way to engage immediately?

Andy Mecca's stepping out to take the baton was itself an invitation—no one wanted to miss their turn at the heroic, and we had already invested greatly—physically, financially, and with our time. We were near the end of the journey. At the beginning of an effort it is different—there is still time to doubt, to waffle, to listen, and admire without engaging. For the leader, this is yet another acid test, the step in message development that is most often skipped, even by the most convincing and passionate leaders. Somehow, many don't believe that it is their right to ask others to act, even on issues that define a company, a country, a family, or an individual.

The internalized doubts are not easy to deal with. "Perhaps I will be ignored. Perhaps no one will show up. Perhaps I will be ridiculed." These concerns are based in reality. Often the visionary is indeed criticized before being praised. The willingness to ask for action in the face of that potential criticism is an unmistakable attribute of leaders. Leaders have the responsibility to spend the necessary contemplative time searching their experience and reviewing the context to gain conviction about the human value of their proposals. It is their responsibility to do the necessary research to become convinced that the evidence supports the decision. They must be willing to act on their own to make this vision come to life. But finally, once heart and mind are in concert, it is their responsibility to clearly call for action on the part of those they are charged to lead.

It takes confidence to act on your own conviction. It takes real courage to ask another human being to do so. The action can be simple and easy to perform, but it must be definitive.

Frequently, a leader does not consider what action other individuals can actually take, and might be satisfied to propose only the organizational steps: a list of sweeping reforms that are far beyond the ability of any single person to effect. Individuals, however, easily become convinced that the issue is too large for their involvement; each believes that "they" will handle the action, so "I" don't have to do anything. Yet the nature of commitment is that it is personal, and it requires an *act* of faith. Asking only for the implementation of a broad-scale and far-reaching agenda redirects the leader's remarks away from the individuals who now share the vision and toward an entity that has no power to commit. Leaders address such requests to "the company," "the department," or "the state" in the name of seeing the big picture—calling for a list of reforms, but unintentionally leaving others with the sense that the problem is just too big for them to act at all. A broad agenda may be appropriate, but if your message is complete and worthy, those who hear it and engage really want to be part of your vision, they want to be part of this new and exciting world you have called for. Asking for a simple, definitive action on their part will test the seal of your bargain, not an agreement to do as they are told, but an agreement to move down a path together. As others perform that simple act, they are affirming their agreement in principle with your proposition, and affirming some level of confidence in your competence and trustworthiness.

John Ure's request was simple:

> Obviously, I can't do this alone. I ask two things of you. First, lay to rest any ghosts you may have of what went before save to learn, and to motivate you towards a more delightful future. Please refrain from attaching blame for the past.

> Second, give positive feedback when you catch people doing things right. In fact, I ask you to come to me in 7 days with 20 things that you have seen from people in this team where you have caught them doing things right. This will set us on our course.

As you might expect, Josie Gaillard's requests regarding gaining oil independence were simple and direct:

> I would ask you to do one of these six things in the next month: Invest in a renewable energy mutual fund, buy power from a green energy provider instead of your local utility, trade your SUV for a convertible energy car, install at least one solar panel at home, write your congressperson about increasing federal emission standards, or tell ten friends why the U.S. addiction to oil must end.

It feels easy enough to do one of those six things, perhaps even two. Both John's and Josie's requests were clearly stated, doable, and relatively easy.

Regardless of the gravity of the situation, offering personal action and asking others for their actions are essential and powerful parts of leadership communication. The very best examples come from situations with the highest stakes.

In the spring of 1948 the leaders of the soon-to-be-born nation of Israel met. They knew the occupying British would soon leave their land and on the day after, eight neighboring states would start a war of annihilation. They needed money—lots of money. David Ben-Gurion, the leader at the time, asked his designated and professional fundraiser to go to the United States. Their goal: to raise another $20 million. "Impossible!" was the reply. "The Americans are tapped out." Golda Meir, not a professional fundraiser but a leader of the Zionists, spoke up and asked to go. She had lived most of her life in Milwaukee and could say, "These are my people."

She was met at the airport by the director of the public relations firm that had been hired to help raise the money. The director asked to see her speech so he could edit it and coach her on its delivery. She told him she had no prepared speech, but that she had reflected for a long time about this issue. It was a life's work. She had an internal guide already composed and completely integrated and she felt strongly she would know exactly what to say when the time came. The public relations man held his breath as she walked onto the stage to address the Council of Jewish Federations, hoping she would not undo all he had been working toward. This is the speech she gave that day.

> Please believe me when I tell you that I have not come to the United States only because several hundred thousand Jews are in danger of being killed. That is not the issue. The issue is that if the Jews of Palestine survive, then the Jews of the world survive with them, and their freedom will be assured forever. But if these several hundred thousand are wiped off the face of the earth, then there will be no Jewish people as such and for centuries to come, all our hopes and dreams of a Jewish nation, a Jewish homeland, will be smashed.
>
> My friends, when I say we need money immediately, I don't mean next week: I mean right now. In less than four months, we will be fighting for our lives against cannon and armor. It is not for you to decide whether we will fight. That decision is taken: we will fight. We will pay for the birth of our nation with our blood. That is normal. The best among us will fall. That is certain. You can decide only one thing: Whether we win or lose.[3]

Obviously, Golda Meir did not need to prepare a speech. She had developed her message over years of involvement and commitment. Everyone knew her competence, most trusted her. All the Jews listening knew the context of this issue: where they had been, where they were, and where they were going. The vision of a Jewish homeland had been shared for more than twenty years. Now it was time to act. Her own commitment was to die, to sacrifice her life. She asked them only for money—and she raised $50 million.

Your own message may not require life-or-death sacrifices, but if you want to lead change, you have to take action and request action.

Will everyone that you talk to act? Of course not. Many will squirm in their metaphorical seats and procrastinate, but keeping the request to act current will keep the engagement temperature at a point where others have to decide, and to finally commit, one way or another. To avoid asking for action is to avoid bringing others to the door of commitment, to avoid requiring that they choose, to avoid risking your own credibility for something in which you believe. Some will act, and those who do will form the first wave of change.

***

Commitment to act, from the organization, from the leader, and from the community of individuals who will effect the change is the last substantive part of the Communication Guide. Once you have completed this part, you can begin to apply what you have developed in the many venues of leadership communication.

Your completed Guide will contain the rudiments of leadership communication. The process of completing it helps you think and, more important, it helps you imagine how you will speak and write about the change you have committed to lead. The Guide's content will appear in every communication you have about this particular issue and the skills of attention and empathy that you have begun to cultivate will bear fruit in every transaction. You'll also discover that the biographical aspects of what you have written are applicable to other facets of your life. You have literally tried to write your Self down on paper.

The final chapter will explore application. I'll demonstrate how the content of the Guide comes into play as you, the leader, begin to deploy the results in a myriad of venues, technologies, and people.

Questions to Ask in Committing to Action

- Organizational and Personal Steps Toward Change
  What steps does the organization need to take to effect the change?
  What is the strength of my personal commitment?
  What specific action am I taking personally regardless of what others may do that is significant enough to inspire them?
- Involving Others—Asking for Commitment
  What specific actions am I going to ask of others to give them a way to engage immediately?
  How can I involve others?
  What can I ask that will give others the chance and the impetus to participate?

Chapter Nine

Leadership Communication in Action

Once you have done the work following the instructions in the previous chapters, you will have undertaken at least two practices. First, you will have discovered and recorded some values and experiences in a new way, and you will have found expression for those values and experiences in the changes that you want to lead. If you are new to the idea of yourself as a leader, it may have come as a surprise that you feel so strongly about something, or that you actually have the capability and interest to lead meaningful change in your family, in your business or other organization, or in your community. If you are presently in a leadership position, then you will have found yourself able to record your change initiatives in a cogent and compelling form, one that is far removed from a briefing book or a white paper. Your message will have progressed from developing trust and displaying competence through demonstrating your commitment to action and involving others. You will have been able to record your purpose, credentials, and personal motivation, your view of context, your dream for the future, and your commitment to act—all of this in a Guide for communicating in a way that will inspire others.

Second, you will have asked questions about others, and in that process of introspection have expanded your awareness of and respect for those you would like to engage. You will have seen leadership's requirements not only as a good idea, a drive to get results, and the competence to make decisions, but also as the ability to build relationships. With this insight, you will have appreciated the need to develop substantial emotional intelligence as a requisite to leading effectively.

Once your change initiative is grounded in insight, personal experience, analogy and metaphor, story, and data, it's time for the next step, for this cause to get in stride with life itself. You need to begin communicating daily with the same awareness that you have displayed in the process of painstakingly developing the Guide. Of course, these processes overlap. As your focus changes and your awareness of leadership communication deepens, you will be making constant modifications and additions to the Guide to further your own and others' understanding and conviction.

These two outcomes are wonderful for me to imagine, and I know that their realization is no mean feat. It is one thing to be able to cite your ideas and feelings on paper; it is another to be able to communicate in real time, frequently with people who don't agree, through the inevitable ups and downs of business cycles and other interruptions, through political crises and unexpected occurrences, through the predictable politics of support and withdrawal of support, the give and take, and the coming and going of fear and doubt—including your own.

I wish I could say that I know someone who does this impeccably, but I don't know any leader who can always, without fail, muster the self-knowledge and control to put the cause before his or her own ego, who somehow always avoids the need for self-aggrandizement and hears others out, acknowledging good faith even when it might not be there and inspiring people to make progress toward a shared goal. I don't know any people who can do that. In other words, I don't know any saints today.

Nonetheless, the goal has to be eminent awareness and flawless execution. Backed by your introspective experience, your knowledge and research, your Guide, and with whatever emotional intelligence you can muster, the depth and clarity of your communication will begin to change. The overarching goal of your communication is to inspire others to take action to effect change. If leadership communication seems a formidable and monumental task to you, remember that it can be broken down into steps, and each step can be practiced and improved. Proactive communication is the easiest, because it can be planned.

Projecting Your Message

In the "push" phase of communication, you first need to decide what medium to use, when to communicate, and how much to communicate. I've related many examples in the text of this book, and this section reviews a few more possibilities for the original declaration as a presentation. Later in the chapter, I share ways to tackle the much more difficult task of responding in real time—the questions after the presentation, informal conversations, and ongoing communication (in a variety of media) about progress. Sometimes it is wise to deploy yourself personally and sometimes alternative channels of communication are acceptable, and it is useful to be able to frame the most effective communication in both cases. The effort you put into preparing your own Communication Guide will reap dividends, regardless of the forum, continually strengthening your connections.

Declaring Possibilities

When a new possibility is declared, when the new reality is introduced, and the effort is ready to launch, usually the first communication is in a speech or presentation. It may not be as noteworthy as Kennedy's charge to go to the moon and back, but it might display many of the same elements. It could be a very public statement or it could be more subtle—a simple message by a business leader to a small group at a retreat or to a board of directors, or a conversation at a family meeting—and it begins the transformation of a group on some scale. I've witnessed both public and more private moments and know that, whatever the forum and without fail, successful leaders who declare change do so only after a great deal of thought, introspection, and crafting, just as the process described in this book suggests.

Not surprisingly, leaders who take the time and energy to discover what matters, work for clarity, enhance emotional intelligence, and connect with others are able to communicate with their authentic voice regardless of the form. Composing a presentation or speech from your Guide gives you every opportunity to avoid arrogance and defensiveness and to display a positive attitude. As you compose, you can explore the history of the issue and look to your human experience for meaning. You can carefully scrutinize the evidence for accuracy and consult with others whom you respect. You can even rehearse your delivery, listening for the sound of authenticity, reworking where necessary to bring your Self forward. You have the opportunity to imagine yourself communicating, whether in front of a camera or live—perhaps with others around the world participating via a web network. It may seem logical to ask for questions and even authentic to do so, but in keeping with your objective of engaging others, it is not always appropriate.

After the Presentation: Is It Time for Engagement?

The three primary considerations in deciding whether to take spontaneous questions are the content of the presentation, the size of the group listening, and whether participants are geographically dispersed. If the discourse is your first advocacy for this change, it is likely to be more abstract and less specific, written to inspire with context and values. Questions could prove frustrating for you and your listeners, and could drain away the excitement that your initial presentation has generated. If your constituency is large or dispersed, taking questions is logistically difficult. The process needs to be tailored to both allow representative questions to be asked and to avoid ill feelings in someone not recognized due to time constraints.

More typically the size of audience and nature of material are not prohibitive, and in such cases you should always offer the chance to clarify, contribute, or challenge your comments. When others can really participate, they are more likely to feel ownership and commitment. In offering to take questions and comments, you are offering a direct relationship to individuals, in addition to the group as a whole. You build expectations of candor in your partners, and can greatly enhance or damage the credibility and trust you have constructed during the presentation and during your tenure as a leader. Your success will depend on how you respond when the questions are finally asked—particularly the tough ones. If you can conduct the question-and-answer period (which will likely extend through the duration of the change effort!) displaying the same competence and connection that were obvious in your more formal remarks, you can further solidify the audience members' trust in you. Doing so requires tapping your emotional intelligence.

Your Internal Conversation—Solicit Questions Authentically

Unless you are speaking at a highly charged political rally, people listening to you will be reluctant to ask questions or make comments that reveal their true objections. This is especially true when you have some formal authority, when others might fear putting themselves at risk in your presence. Most people will not call attention to themselves by being negative about a change, particularly after the first presentation, or perhaps even for the first few months of a change effort. You must connect to get people to open up. This skill may not be foremost in your mind after a presentation. Instead, many leaders have a commentary similar to the following running in their brains: "Now I'm finished. I hope someone doesn't ask a stupid question or raise an objection in front of this group. Let's just get on with it. I don't want to have to prove my point over and over."

Remember that people are unconsciously aware of intention, so even if this musing remains unsaid, it nonetheless comes across. Worse, even if questions are asked, convention makes it easy to evade the unpleasant. It is not comfortable to deal with anger, disappointment, or disagreement. It is tempting to treat questions and comments as though the intent of the commentator is stated only in the words. A leader will rarely be criticized for ignoring indirect challenges. Here is the unspoken bargain: The questioner hides the intent to avoid direct confrontation; the leader detects the illusion and ignores it to avoid dealing with the real issue. This is an insidious agreement. Authenticity demands that this bargain not be kept. The first to acknowledge the real agenda gains the respect and admiration of others.

Leaders who truly want commitment will solicit feedback in a way that frees people from those shackles of fear, knowing that each question or comment that is authentic will help free others who might otherwise not be willing to be heard. How do you do it? By having a different internal conversation, and then making it external. For example, if you were a leader standing in front of your constituents, you might be thinking these thoughts, saying these words:

> Now you've heard what I have to say and why I think this is the best way to change in order to get to where we want to go. I'm sure there are reservations. I would be amazed if there aren't some concerns about job security, whether your hours will change, how this change will affect you personally. I'm sure also that some of you disagree with this course of action. While I've done the best I can, solicited the best advice, and thought this through thoroughly, I'm not infallible, and there is still room for some adjustments for things we did not consider.
>
> I don't have all the details worked out yet, and in fact am counting on all of you to help in that. That includes the asking of questions or the making of comments in this hall, right now, that will bring the real concerns to the surface. I'll do my best to respond.
>
> Some of you might be thinking that expressing disagreement or insecurity would be an affront to me, and that you might be putting yourself in jeopardy. Some of you may have perceived others in similar situations who suffered because of an ill-timed question. But we need commitment, not mere compliance with this change. Please ask questions or make comments that are real, so that we can move ahead with the course of action that is best for all of us.
>
> While it is best that we air as much as we can together, if you would rather not ask or comment in this forum, or if you think of something after we leave, or if we just don't have time to take all of your thoughts or concerns here, I invite you to use my e-mail box or just come and see me.

This is the same introspective process you used in developing your Communication Guide: acknowledging resistance and showing your motivation and vulnerabilities. It develops trust, and it takes the conversation to a new level of resonance. The first time you make these comments, you might draw some skeptics. But if you persevere, others will start to contribute. This kind of honesty fosters commitment.

Whether another's question or comment is made immediately after a presentation or as part of another interaction, your response also demands emotional intelligence.

Listening and Responding with Emotional Intelligence

As discussed in Chapter Two, emotional intelligence means *recognition, resonance, regulation,* and *response.* None of these may arise naturally or immediately when you are questioned or challenged. Instead, each conversation could become a new battle to be won, each question a new threat to your cause and, more honestly, to your ego. In these moments, you could forget that you are a leader of a cause and instead become a defensive warrior, attacking with your passion, your authority, your position, and your command of the data. In your words and your stance, you dare anyone to say anything. Not surprisingly, they don't. Emotional intelligence helps by offering options that can lead to inclusion rather than exclusion and that create connection rather than opposition.

The following pages set out guidelines for soliciting questions and responding to them after a speech, or in any other less-formal interchange. The process recalls the questions posed in helping you develop your Communication Guide.

Responding Authentically to Question and Intent

Many questions are really two questions: the stated one that is literal, and the unstated one that is only pointed to by the words or emphases in the comment or question. Your first task is to discern when the stated and unstated questions coincide and when they don't. Your second task is to respond to both. In doing so, you display competence and can generate a new level of trust.

The stated question is obvious, conveyed by the words the questioner uses; the unstated one may only be revealed in the subtleties of the voice, body posture, and attitude of the questioner. The former is the objective question; the latter is the intent of the questioner. While they can be congruent, in cases of disagreement, they rarely are. Each question carries with it the background and knowledge of the questioner and the context of the subject matter itself. As you learn to be more discerning under the spotlight of questions, it can be helpful to think about questions in categories: contributions, requests for clarification, and disputes or challenges.

Contributions may be voiced as questions, but are comments of support. The questioner wants to be heard as sympathetic (the unstated intent) and elects to elaborate on the positive nature of one of the points of your speech by giving additional evidence or examples. If you agree that the example or experience of the questioner is appropriate, such contributions are easy to handle.

Questions for information and clarification are also relatively easy and not stressful. The stated and unstated questions are the same, and there are generally no negative feelings associated with the question. The questioner merely missed a point or wants some clarification about what you said.

You can handle contributions and requests for information easily by acknowledging the question, commenting or clarifying, and confirming that you have been responsive. These three steps are fundamental in responding to every inquiry.

However, many questions or comments rendered in change processes are neither contributions nor requests for clarification. They are *disputes or challenges,* and are often disguised in the rhetorical clothes of the other categories. The stated and unstated questions are not the same. For example, "I was having trouble hearing you from the back of the room. I believe you said that the company would save $4 million in the first year of this change. Is that the correct number?" *could* be a simple request for clarification—depending upon how it's said. Or it might be rephrased as "I believe you said that the company would save $4 million in the first year of this change, but *I couldn't believe my ears.* Is that the correct number?" This brings the dispute to the foreground and is clearly something more. Whether the message is literal or conveyed subtly, each requires a different response.

"How many people will relocate to Detroit to accomplish the transfer of work?" is a request for more information. "How many people will *have to move* to Detroit to accomplish the transfer of work?" might carry disenchantment with the request. The changes in wording or even in energy signal a change in the intent of the question. It's quite possible that the questioner would make the intent less obvious. The question might be couched in the original words, but with a voice full of cynicism. Perhaps the questioner is sitting hunched over, arms folded. But is the posture an indication of defiance or physical chill? Here's where all your powers of observation and emotional intelligence come into play. Disputes and challenges are rich in opportunity and risk. They call for maximum awareness and skill on the part of the leader. Even the body language consultants can't give effective rules. You simply have to be aware of intent. Just as explained in Chapter Two, even experts in interpreting signals might miss some clues. Still, trust your intuition and ask. You will usually be correct, and even if you are not, your respondent will appreciate your interest and sensitivity.

Anticipating Questions and Feelings

The construction of your Guide includes anticipating both emotional and logical resistance, and during the initial verbalization of the needed change, you will be foreshadowing such issues. Nonetheless, it helps to prepare mentally for questions you anticipate. When you do so, consider not only the question itself but the feelings that might accompany the question, or perhaps might be the basis for asking the question in the first place.

I was present at a quarterly employee presentation of earnings for a large global company. During the preparation time for the presentation, my client mentioned that he had planted a question in the small group that would be attending the presentation in person. In this particular company, every employee bonus (with the important exception of the officers') was calculated using a rubric for "Return on Invested Capital." This measurement, while critical to stockholders and perhaps to the Board of Directors, is frequently anathema to employees themselves, in that ROIC is a function of both profit and investment. Accordingly, any time a company makes an acquisition of any size, it has a dramatic effect on the return. In general, employees other than officers don't have much input on decisions to invest in major acquisitions. This particular year, the company had acquired a large competitor, and even though the year's earnings had been outstanding, the size of the investment pushed ROIC substantially below the norm. Accordingly, the employees' bonuses were going to be paid at only 50 percent of potential, while the officers were going to be paid a much higher percentage of their potential bonus. Everyone knew this going into the meeting, and my client wanted to get it out into the open. For this, I applauded him.

The question didn't need to be planted. Immediately after my client's presentation on the outstanding profit numbers for the quarter, a gentleman in the front row raised the question. With a lot of zeal in his voice, he asked, "Why did we only get a 50 percent bonus payout when the company had such a great quarter?" My client immediately went into an explanation of the formula used in the calculation of the bonus. The questioner was not satisfied, of course, but pursued it with a question about the level of bonus for the executives (which my client answered truthfully, again trying to differentiate the formulas). The dialogue ended with bad feelings, as one might anticipate.

What beneficial outcome might have resulted had the client employed the reach of emotional intelligence? Had my client recognized the questioner's emotions, he could have resonated with the questioner, regulated his own defensiveness, and responded accordingly:

> It sounds like you are upset about this, and I can understand. We obviously had a great profit year. Because the bonus is calculated on return on investment, our large acquisition had a short-term adverse effect on the numbers, and that is what made the payout what it was. Because the officers are paid bonuses on a broader base of measurements, it didn't affect our numbers as dramatically. I understand how this might seem unfair to you. I can tell you for sure that if the investment decision was correct, then it will result in greater earnings and a much bigger payout of bonuses in the future.

This response would have at least acknowledged the feelings and demonstrated that the executive understood the questioner's point of view. Ultimately, of course, one has to question the wisdom of not making an exception in the bonus payout for that particular year, perhaps averaging the ROIC portion of the formula over the subsequent two years. Barring that action, displaying the emotional intelligence to acknowledge the feelings would have mitigated the negative atmosphere and maintained a trusting atmosphere in the room.

Hear the Person, Not Merely the Question

William Miller, a close friend and consultant, told me a story of working with an executive of a Texas company. This man was known as an autocrat, but he was exceptionally bright and extremely competent. To gain a benchmark for working with him, William suggested a 360-degree instrument that would solicit feedback from his direct reports. Before the feedback was complete, William asked the executive how he believed his subordinates would rate him as a listener. He responded, "I think they will say I'm a bad listener, but if you press them, they will say that I always understand their content." The executive made this comment with the belief that his subordinates didn't understand what real listening was, that their response to the second question would prove that he was effective.

He was exactly right in his prediction. What he didn't understand was that listening is not so much about data as it is about empathy and inspiration. "Did he get your content?" is a different question from "Did you feel heard?" The former deals with the mind, the latter, with the emotions, and people will rarely trust someone who responds only to facts, never to them, leaving them feeling unimportant.

This Texas leader confused the need to answer questions with the need to respond to people. Yet anyone in a relationship has confronted this difference, and might have learned that both are necessary. Particularly when dealing with change or inspiration, responding to the person will lead to much better results, even if the question itself isn't answered with technical correctness.

In Chapter Two, I suggested that empathy—acknowledging others and acknowledging their points of view—was central to developing trust, and that trust has to be developed before commitment can take place. The same idea is true in soliciting and answering questions. Building trust is our first goal.

Invested Listening: A Summary

Like developing the message itself, applying a simple framework to your responses to challenges can help you train yourself away from defensiveness and nonproductive communication.

Defensiveness erodes trust. If you can find agreement with the questioner and respond to both the intent of the question and the feelings of the questioner, you can continue to earn the faith of others, and you can make your communication productive. Once you become really invested in hearing the intent of the other person, you have a chance of gaining agreement and even commitment. The invested listening model has five primary elements:

- Hearing and answering the stated and unstated question
- Acknowledging feelings
- Finding common intent
- Distinguishing between your context, or point of view, and the questioner's point of view
- Checking in: making sure that you have been responsive

Listening perceptively to your constituents and discovering what's underlying their stated comments is important, but you need to respond in a way that connects with your listeners and shows them that you have truly heard them. By acknowledging their common intent, their concerns, and their context in addition to their stated comments, you can build an environment for trust and openness. You also open the possibility for further innovation related to the change, since your constituents may indeed have ideas and insights, based on their unique experience, that would improve upon the effectiveness of the plan you are suggesting. Your challenge is to balance inquiry with advocacy. You have to convey not only that you are open to input about how to achieve results but also that you are committed to moving the vision forward.

At a conference on illegal drug use in New York, the primary speaker advocated spending more federal money on drug treatment services. She entertained a question from a listener who immediately agreed with the speaker's context, and went on to suggest the abolition of the federal drug enforcement effort. The questioner finished with an endorsement of drug legalization.

The instinctive response would have been to defend against the subtle attack: "I don't believe that legalization is an answer to the drug problem. I think it is shortsighted, sends the wrong signal to the wrong population at the wrong time, and would kill far more of our young people than the current rash of drug violence." That answer might be technically correct from the speaker's point of view, but it is only responsive to the disagreement with the questioner. Had the speaker confirmed the common ground with the questioner (the context of the problem), acknowledged the feelings that were present (frustration and anger), and then made the distinction in their positions (legalization versus treatment), she could have maintained mutual respect and reinforced her own solution. For example:

> I appreciate your support for an increase in our investment in treatment. But I also hear your deep dissatisfaction with the drug enforcement effort and our level of federal spending to support that activity. Your comments reflect the frustration of many who see drug crime continue to rise with an ever-increasing death toll among our young. I share that frustration.
>
> While we seem to agree that increased treatment will have an impact on those already addicted, I believe it would be bad policy to signal to our youth that illicit drugs in any quantity would be appropriate to use. I believe, in fact, that the enforcement effort over the years has been a holding action, effective at maintaining pressure on supply while we have been developing our understanding of demand reduction strategies. The next few years of a more *balanced* approach of supply and demand reduction should yield even better results.

This response emphasizes the area of agreement, acknowledges the feelings of the questioner, and still makes the distinction in the two positions. The key elements are first, speaking to the common ground and second, openly acknowledging the intensity and opinion of the questioner. Like openly acknowledging resistance in the beginning of a speech, these aspects of the answer can deepen the connection between the listener and questioner, and can signal a level of safety to the rest of those who hear the exchange, or who hear of the exchange later.

Another example: At a town hall meeting of two hundred senior managers in the southwest United States, the popular, well-respected CEO was entertaining questions. He had spoken earlier about a bright future for the company and had implored everyone to look to both revenue enhancements and cost savings in their respective operations. This was a public company and the CEO's annual salary and bonuses had been posted in the paper the previous week—in seven figures. The latest quarter's performance had been good, but not fantastic.

The question came from a field manager. The tone was very flat and noncommittal: "Uh, I have an employee who is the backbone of our operation. She comes in early in the morning, stays late at night, takes the initiative to solve customer problems, and is the cheerleader for the rest of the office. Her job classification doesn't qualify her for stock options in our company. Now you make a lot of money, much more than I do, and"—the field manager paused for a split second, before continuing—"I'm sure you deserve it. What are we doing about passing the opportunity for options down to employees like her?"

As a consultant, I was seated in the back of the room calmly attending to the questions. By contrast, the CEO was seated on a stool on the stage with bright lights in his eyes. He was faced with responding in a cogent way while keeping up appearances. The stated question was a request for information: "Are we going to lower the requirements for employees to qualify for stock options?" The unstated concern was to call into question the pay scale of the executive. The feelings were resentment and probably some anger. The real question was a challenge: "Why do you make so much money when the rest of us do all the work?" Unsophisticated, perhaps, or even immature, but real. At some level of consciousness, everyone in the room heard the real question.

The CEO launched into an answer to the stated question, reviewing the history of the option plan, reminding the audience of the many ways employees could gain ownership in the company and explaining why the option plan was reserved for employees of a certain level. When he was finished, he asked the questioner if he had answered the question. The questioner said, "I guess so," and left it at that. This CEO did exactly what most of us would do, only he did it slightly better.

Later, I reviewed the meeting with the CEO. When I came to this question, I asked him if he had heard anything more than the literal question. I played the question back from the recording, and he remembered the split second when he had heard everything: the words, the intent, and the feelings. In less than 200 milliseconds, his amygdala had taken over and he had reacted with his answer, following his underlying instinct to protect, defend, and justify.

We reviewed other possibilities, and decided on this one:

> Tom has asked about our reasons for limiting stock options to directors and above, but I hear some other concerns in his question as well, concerns that go to the issue of executive compensation in relationship to the pay of others. In case I'm right about that, I want to respond to those issues as well. *(Respond to the stated question and the common intent.) (Acknowledge the feeling and the unstated concern.)*
>
> First, on the issue of options. We have found over time that employees below a certain pay level use options only as compensation. They execute their options and cash them in right away. The purpose of any stock ownership plan is to encourage people who work in the company to have a real stake in the company's performance. So we think that the opportunities that we have to purchase stock in 401(k) programs accomplish that purpose. Above and beyond that, everyone can buy stock at a discount through the stock purchase plan, and there are no restrictions on how long you must hold that stock. Does that respond to that part of your question, Tom? *(Answer the stated question.)*
>
> Now, to the larger issue of executive compensation, I want you to know that I appreciate anyone who cares enough about the company to be concerned about this, and I particularly admire his courage in asking me that question. He pointed out that the real heart of this company is in employees like the one he described, people like you who come to work in the branches every day and interface directly with our customers. I know and appreciate that, as does every member of the executive team. If we aren't telling you that enough, then we need to get out more. *(Answer the unstated question.)*

> The whole issue of executive compensation is the subject of much publicity right now, and Tom's question gives me a reason to speak to it directly. I have an interest, as you do, in making sure that our company is spending its compensation dollars in the best possible way.
>
> As some of you know, executive compensation is set by the board of directors, specifically by a committee of outside directors. We set it up this way to avoid any appearance of being self-serving, and to assure that we emphasize long-term results rather than short-term movement in the stock price. That means that the officers are paid the bulk of their compensation on the basis of long-term objectives and a smaller portion on year-to-year operations. For a company in our stage of development, that seems like the right course to me. (*Distinguish between their context and yours.*)
>
> The compensation committee also assures that we are competitive in our industry, so that the officers aren't moving to competitive firms because we were shortsighted. In all, the process seems correct, but it is certainly a process that is open for any of you to inquire about further.
>
> This morning, I talked about the need for all of us to improve our revenue stream and control costs. Those objectives are in keeping with our plan for more long-term investment next year in order to fuel what we see as dramatic growth. At the end of our five-year plan, I believe we will all see that the investments we are making now in compensation will have been well-placed and that they will result in greater opportunity for all of us. I hope that is responsive to that issue, Tom. And again, I appreciate your bringing it up. (*Check in.*)

This was obviously easier to compose after the fact. We did not use it as a revision for the questioner. Rather, constructing this answer was part of coaching the CEO to respond more authentically the next time he was confronted with a similar situation. In contrast to the more leisurely development of the Communication Guide itself, the question-and-answer session requires your attention in split seconds and in public. Practice and review can provide you with the reminders you need to respond more effectively in the future.

Challenges and disputes, whether hidden and subtle or open and aggressive, present opportunities for new levels of engagement with the others. As you learn to listen (and observe) more attentively and intuitively to your own emotional responses and those of others, and as you invest the courage it takes to acknowledge what you hear (and see), you create an atmosphere of trust and openness. Using elements of the invested listening model will help you achieve interactions that are clearer and deeper, more connected and more candid. You will, as a result, get real engagement rather than mere lip service or conventional responses. Like the sequence suggested for the speech itself, these steps act as a map toward an authentic response. Practicing them will make you more thoughtful, less defensive, and more responsive to others.

The Daily Practice of Leadership Communication

When we think of delivering a significant change or initiative, a speech or presentation is the application that most often comes to mind. However, it is in the far more frequent informal and spontaneous conversations—in the town halls, meetings, and one-to-one conversations that take place in conference rooms, offices, and around the coffee machine—that leadership is most often practiced. To be effective as a leader you must over time bring yourself authentically, in your real skin, to the full range of situations in which you will be called to move your advocacy forward.

All your communications can and should be built on the foundation of core ideas that comprise your Guide. Who you are and what you care about does not change in the course of moving from formal speaking to casual conversation—although finding the courage to express the reality of your humanness may come more easily in one venue than in the other. In informal conversations and discussions, of course, all of this must happen in real time. In the face of questions, contributions, and challenges, the natural human tendency is to defend ourselves, patronize the listeners, avoid personal exposure, and make the point with even greater certainty. In the process, unfortunately, this sort of reaction drives wedges that make it difficult for others to speak with honesty or candor in our presence.

To gain support for a change, it's more important to know how to create an environment in which people feel safe to honestly express real thoughts and feelings, including disagreements, than it is to deliver a speech with authenticity, clarity, and heart. It takes discipline and practice to stay authentic regardless of the situation, consistently interacting in a way that engenders trust and inspires commitment. Having made the decision to lead, you have a responsibility to extend yourself beyond your immediate emotional response to one that includes empathy for others. This is not always easy. In fact, it is rarely easy. But if you are going to lead, it is essential.

These dynamics come into play in informal settings far more frequently than in formal presentations. Soliciting and answering questions and generating proactive communication through other media are common events for leaders of change, and were covered in the text. These situations lend themselves to practice, models, and rules. In many ways, the leader can observe these situations, reflect, and react appropriately. More difficult are the casual and spontaneous conversations that include some objection, emotional or logical, to the change. These encounters can happen in informal atmospheres when you have something else on your mind. They are difficult in that they catch you when you are prone to react rather than respond. Pressure situations require a higher level of consciousness, an extra breath to allow the amygdala to disengage.

Interacting in Person, Proactively

In addition to answering questions and having dialogue, a leader communicates proactively, purposely reminding others of progress and lack of it, cheering and cajoling, measuring and asking for feedback. Much of this communication simply must be done in person. Perhaps the most difficult is actually assessing the performance of others. These interactions are hard to accomplish objectively while still responding to the emotional content.

Evaluation and coaching the performance of others is a key element of a leader's role—not just the formal annual performance appraisal that is common in business but the regular and informal feedback that shapes day-to-day behavior. Being able to candidly let individuals know how they are performing and then offer suggestions for change requires a level of interpersonal skill. This is particularly true during major change, as people tend to drag their feet or need reinforcement from the leader to continue the process.

Not surprisingly, performance measurement is reported as the most onerous communication required of business leaders, particularly during times of rapid change. It is the forced breaking of convention—it is a time in which we are supposed to tell the truth in order to rate someone's performance and help them improve. But few want to do that. In business, companies struggle with getting appraisals completed on time, and when they do, they struggle with compression at the top of the curve, with far more people being rated "A" or "exceeds requirements" than "D" or "needs substantial improvement." As a result, when a person's performance deteriorates to a level that requires corrective action, or when a reduction in force requires that a company lay off the weakest performers, few leaders and few employees are prepared. The weaker performers have not been told the truth, so not infrequently, the person fired has been told, in sequence, "good," "good," and "goodbye!" This "good" "good," is the equivalent of social promotion in the school system, and like that phenomenon, has a detrimental impact on everyone. The person fired has not been given honest feedback that might have sparked real improvement. The leader has shirked the responsibility to develop the employees. Those remaining feel their fired coworker was treated unfairly. (And they are right.) They also may begin to doubt the importance of their own good appraisal, and fear that they might be the next to go.

How could an appraisal be conducted using the models offered here? Listen to this leader introduce the process to one of his direct reports:

> Tom, this appraisal is a ritual that we perform on a regular basis, and sometimes it can be a difficult one. It really helps if we keep the purpose in mind. We're here to make sure that you and I see eye-to-eye on your performance, and to help you to continue to improve and develop so you can grow your career. (*Stating the purpose of the communication an the commonly desired change.*)
>
> I wouldn't be surprised if you were nervous about it. Sometimes being graded doesn't feel so good. Truthfully, in the past, this has not been my favorite activity either, but as soon as I can see it as a chance to help you rather than a chore I have to perform, I feel differently about it. That point of view also helps me see any criticism I might offer as constructive rather than hurtful or personal. It is my intent to be helpful in this process, not just to give my personal opinion of how you've done. (*Acknowledging feelings, admitting vulnerability, distinguishing between the employee's context —criticism—and the leader's—support. Pointing to commonali —desire for improvement.*)
>
> What I thought we could do is review briefly where we've been, take a look at your plan from last year, our expectations that we set down, then review where we are, how you've performed against the benchmarks, and then spend some time looking to the future—where you want to go. Then at the end, we can make some commitments to one another about what we are going to do for the next period. How does that sound? (*Establishing the framework, asking for the other's point of view— empathy.*)

This lead-in conversation sets up the framework discussion. The leader has established some trust by being clear about purpose, acknowledging some resistance, and relating personal motivation. Then he has suggested that the two create a shared context by reviewing the "story" as they have both seen it, which will be the main part of the appraisal. He has also suggested a look to the future, and the certainty of making commitments to one another to help bring that future about. If the leader is able to direct the conversation, maintaining his emotional control, the interview can result in a positive outcome for both. This conversation follows the framework of the Personal Leadership Communication Guide.

Not in Person but Still Personal

Aside from formal evaluation, nearly every other kind of leadership communication can be done electronically, *but only after you have earned the privilege; only after the recipients know you and trust you.* In a stunning article in the *Harvard Business Review,* Edward Hallowell warns, "The human moment is disappearing from modern life, and I sense that we all may be about to discover the destructive power of its absence."[1] Only in your presence can recipients of your communication fill in any literal ambiguity from their personal experience of who you are. Whatever form these messages take, the key element is your deployment of your Self; your commitment to be satisfied only with inspiration rather than information. If you have been face-to-face with those you are e-mailing or texting, the ambiguity can be dissipated. In the absence of any sense of who you are, individuals will typically, Hallowell says, "revert to the most negative scenario."

During change efforts, proactive messages are critical to progress, as others are constantly reassessing, asking themselves: Why are we doing this? What is my role? Am I secure here or not? Does the leader have a grip on what's happening? All this uncertainty can be allayed, but not with information alone. Rather than needing only rational explanations to commit, most people need emotional reinforcement. This is the leader's charge, to maintain a leadership perspective in all communication throughout the process, in every proactive change communication that takes place, even electronic communication. Having said that, Tom Lewis, co-author of *A General Theory of Love,* opines that a well-written letter or e-mail can be more effective in transmitting empathy than an impersonal face-to-face encounter.[2]

The more people know you personally, the more likely they are to fill in whatever they need to make your message effective on both these levels. To test the truth of this statement, imagine an e-mail from a new HR executive telling you that he wants to discuss your job performance with you, versus the same words, same format from your boss of five years. One creates anxiety, the other seems much more routine and less threatening. Spouses who have lived together for thirty years barely have to talk to understand one another. Lawyers in a courtroom have to cover every detail. One communication requires practically no context, and the other requires very high context; every word must be defined.

Ross Dove was founding CEO of DoveBid, a California company that assembled industrial assets no longer being used and auctioned them off. It operated around the world. Ross is an animated and thoughtful leader who communicates well and often. During the early days of his company he traveled worldwide, visiting the more than seven hundred employees personally twice a year. Once a quarter, Ross drafted a "Chairman's letter" and distributed it by e-mail to his entire company. If he did this every day, or even once a week, it's possible that no one would read it. But once a quarter, everyone looked forward to it. Notice the elements that he covers in this excerpt.

> A Chairman's e-mail in mid-August . . . Ugh! I'm fresh back from vacation and hope you are all having a great summer and have also enjoyed some time off. Like most of you, I don't realize how tired I get and how much I need to recharge my batteries until about the third day away from calls and e-mail. The good news is by about the seventh day, I can't wait to get back in the game because I don't think there is a job on earth more fun than this one.
>
> After a dozen Chairman's letters, I thought I would give you all a break from vision 2010 and my "Knute Rockne" pump up speeches. Instead, I find myself in a more reflective mood and ask you to stop, take a breath and spend a moment with me to enjoy what we have already accomplished together. Today, we have a company where many of us have become great friends and partners and just like my eighteen-year-old son says to his friends, "Don't worry, I've got your back," I believe a lot of us are beginning to feel exactly that. We can now count on, lean on, and trust each other to be loyal to the enterprise and the vision and to truly admit and acknowledge our success will come from every one of us doing our part and helping the next guy look and feel good.

Of course, the greatest challenge ahead is to set a high standard for that culture and live up to it. The greatest challenge I find personally is that with 700 people, every day I am bombarded with more and more information . . . good and bad. The bigger you are the more deals you win and ironically the more deals you lose. The bigger you are the more support and compliments you get as well as more criticism. One of the most interesting criticisms I have been receiving is that DoveBid is becoming too competitive internally. I have been told that there is a great deal of focus on salespeople competing with each other rather than with our competitors. That there is interdepartmental competition for promotions and that some people believe all of this has raised a level of tension in our enterprise. It is a good criticism and one I will need your help with.

Simply stated, we win when our clients win and our clients win when they get the best possible representation from DoveBid. Each of us has different skill sets and we are stronger together. In all companies, this is a challenge and it cannot be resolved with rules. It must be resolved with the golden rule. If everybody comes together with the belief that ultimate equity comes from constantly striving to be fair, then sound and good business judgment will always be the deciding factor. We all know the very best athletes are always gracious in both victory and defeat and they are really most passionate about effort. We all need to address this issue, and I know it can't be done by e-mail alone. So with a little luck, I'll be planning and executing two roadshows, one to the institutions, followed by an around-the-world trip to come see every one of you.

Ross starts by acknowledging some potential resistance (Ugh!), then lets them know his motivation: it is a letter of gratitude. He introduces the problem of competition, tells a story of a similar situation (not included in the extract here), and suggests the solution. He then asks for their help and makes a commitment.

Because Ross traveled extensively, because he provided every employee with some experience of knowing him, these employees had come to view his e-mailed chairman's letters as notes from home. They knew him. They knew his intention and understood it. Ross had earned the right to communicate in this way by deploying himself personally. People in his company filled in the blanks of intention, even when Ross forgot, because he forgot so infrequently.

The next example is another e-mail from a Fortune 500 CEO that follows a personal announcement about the need to restructure, a difficult message.

> Today, I'm announcing further steps in the difficult but necessary process of restructuring our company to succeed in this extremely challenging business environment. While I spoke to all of you yesterday about this, I want to reiterate some of what I said.
>
> First, this is necessary because of the changing needs of our clients, and our commitment to continue our heritage of providing the services and products that they find most useful. As the leader in moving the industry in new directions, we simply have to be the most responsive; keeping our clients, our shareholders, and most of all, you, confident of our long-term success.
>
> Obviously this is not easy. Our messages may feel contradictory sometimes. It may appear we are both going forwards and backwards at the same time. In some sense this is true. Even as we charge ahead with new capabilities and offerings that are attracting attention and winning in the marketplace, we also have to go backwards and clean up some of the over-capacity we built in the past for a different era.

The second note went on to cover more specifics, but the leader first reiterated what he had said personally, and then once again, acknowledged some obvious resistance, that the messages might seem contradictory, growing in some areas, but shrinking in others. Because this leader had addressed the issues personally, he could use e-mail to support his change process.

The same rules demonstrated in the two e-mail messages can be applied to other kinds of indirect communication. Consider carefully what the listeners might not know, or might not remember, rather than assuming that they know and accept everything. Also be sure to include your own motivation (even if it means reiterating it).

Electronic communication (including voice mail, e-mail, Web meetings, video, teleconferencing, and more) to support your change efforts is only as effective as your ability to continue to deploy your Self as well as provide information. These media are once-removed from human contact, and as such, they can seem sterile and inflexible. Still, if you as leader have established your trustworthiness and competence personally, by deploying yourself generously with those you wish to inspire, these modes can be used effectively to reinforce your message.

Follow-up conversation, performance appraisal, and electronic reinforcement are all inevitable in change initiatives. They call for the leader's best—self-awareness, self-control, and empathy. With these three, even the most difficult and complex communication can be productive.

***

Regardless of the form a communication takes—a speech, a town hall meeting, an informal conversation, an e-mail, or any other—your overriding responsibility as a leader is to be present in the communication, rather than being beside it. Authenticity is the bridge from compliance to commitment, from satisfaction to loyalty, from mere change to progress, and as I said at the outset, it is the critical element in inspiration. Interactions are multiplying, but they needn't lose their personal meaning. For the aware, every interaction is a chance to deploy the Self, to further progress in whatever world in which you live.

Epilogue
Communication: The Cauldron of Leadership

The sole measure of real leadership is how others are affected by the leader's character, vision, and action. Central to all of these is communication, specifically *leadership* communication, the skill that is most essential for leaders to be effective. What I've suggested in these pages is that the practice of authentic leadership communication has been slowly waning, even as the need for it is becoming greater. Particularly in the public and business arenas, we find more and more posturing fueled by selfish objectives—whether money, power, or both. With the erosion of authenticity, trust—in our leaders and in the institutions they represent—has plummeted. The rebellious activity currently rampant in the world is a direct result of what many see to be self-serving manipulative behavior on the part of people in power.

Worse, due to the proliferation of media sources from broadcast and the Internet, we are becoming used to judging appearance rather than substance, a habit that allows us to pretend we don't need the authentic. Still, when it does show up, when a leader communicates in a way that inspires us, we recognize it immediately: we know that we are not being merely entertained, and we are drawn in.

One result of this paucity is a belief that the power to change things should reside in the populace as a whole. This is, in some ways, a wonderful vision, but it does smack of a utopian world society where everyone has the same information and enjoys the same perspective. Unfortunately, this is just not true . . . everyone does not have access to the information that might be most important. I don't all believe that the answer to progress lies in a process of groupthink or the world voting via social media on every issue or policy. We just don't all have—and we don't all pay attention to—the same information.

The truth is that some among us have a broader perspective, and all of us have the *capacity* to develop such a perspective. Real leaders call us to our higher angels, who fly substantially above the mob. In this environment of interdependency, progress depends on those who have global values, who can envision change on a global scale and who can communicate effectively to an ever-widening diverse population, understanding and including others, modeling cooperation and common values, and knowing when to take a stand. The requisite skills are the same as those needed to sustain any individual relationship, but for the leader the stakes are larger and the impact greater.

Organizational leaders who foster joint commitment to meaningful endeavor will excel. National leaders who hold fast to values and substance will gain support. Those who still depend on engendering passive compliance through manipulation will eventually falter. It is the energy of collective conviction that will fuel answers to the complex questions of global competition, national social malaise, fanatical extremism, and the quandary of international cooperation.

People make commitments to causes they value and to people they respect and trust. Rediscovering an authentic voice and maintaining a commitment to meaningful change are requisites for any leader who would respond to these needs. Such authenticity requires that you communicate from both mind and heart, directly to the minds and hearts of others. When those who listen sense both competence and connection, they are willing to engage, to consider their own commitment, and eventually, to act.

Ideas can be learned from others, but passion lives in personal experience. Just as John Gardner suggested thirty years ago in *Self-Renewal,* the first step to creating change in any venue is to continually reaffirm what is personally meaningful by reflecting on the actual shaping events of our lives. As leaders, increasing knowledge of internal truth has to be a central theme, and will, as a discipline, tend to deepen all of our messages. Perhaps that deepening can slake today's technological thirst to make shallow messages more broadly heard.

Technology can replace all parts of the body, but it cannot synthesize the whisper of the human spirit. By paying attention to those most important urgings, we can amplify that whisper to an audible call. Having thus re-experienced our own conviction, we can begin to bring it to others. I've implored discipline in this work. I've asked for contemplation and for the writing of possibility, as these disciplines will quiet the voices, external or internal, that might have an agenda of quick and parochial intent.

We've learned from history that all change starts from a stirring in some individual human soul. We also know that communication is the life-blood of relationship. From the first image of possibility to the first word on paper or the first utterance of wonder, the ultimate outcome of a change being fully and finally manifested, you as leader can become a vehicle to carry others to decision and commitment. By including both facts and feelings, by exposing both credentials and personal qualities, and by entering into the interaction with others honestly and completely, you can offer real meaning in addition to the objective rewards of shared accomplishment.

Because we humans are out of the practice of being real, because the veil of conventional, civilized behavior lies lightly upon us and is easily parted—particularly when the ideas and initiatives we value deeply are questioned or challenged—I have offered some frameworks that will encourage the use of both objective and subjective evidence, that will engage you as well as those you inspire. But because authenticity depends on your intent, the only guarantee of success will come from your own subscription to these ideas and your dedication to rekindling that intent each time you communicate, whatever the form.

I know from experience that consciousness doesn't come easily; it comes in hard-earned billionths of a second. But there are ways of training ourselves to expand those moments to full seconds, minutes, hours, and sometimes days. When we communicate authentically, we add immensely to the possibility for others to do the same, and for real leadership to once again emerge in the human family and to defeat cynicism one encounter at a time.

I realize too, that the *gotcha* world of the media has made authenticity more frightening, particularly to public figures, but even to the most stalwart of souls without perceived exposure. There may be a price to pay in terms of ridicule by those who can't match your courage, but that *is* the price of leadership. Authentic does not mean indecisive, vulnerable does not mean weak, and we need not abandon the mind to listen to the heart.

It takes work to remember that we are connected first as human beings, rather than only through our roles. In our lives of planning and executing, the reality of our humanness and its inseparability from the parts we play rarely surfaces unless we make time and develop a discipline to see it. This book is meant to encourage you to take that time, to provide a discipline for you to use, and to implore you to actively and authentically communicate your discovery to others. Those you lead will be richer and more successful for it, as will you.

Appendixes

Appendix A

The Choice and Use of Evidence in Leadership Communication

In the text, I stress the point that leadership communication is both clear and deep. Because generally, we are better at communicating the clear part than the deep part, I've said little about evidence in the text. But there are some principles of evidence that, when followed, can add immensely to the understanding and receptivity of others.

Chapter Six includes an example from a speech by John Adams. The evidence he uses about the need for corporate emphasis on family issues was clear:

> Fewer than 22 percent of married-couple households consists of a male breadwinner and female homemaker. In the 1950s, the figure was 80 percent. Fifty-eight percent of mothers with children under six now hold paying jobs. The figure was 20 percent in 1960. And 68 percent of mothers with children under 18 work outside the home.

This evidence was cited as part of the historical context and is well done, but data can also help show the size of a problem, forecast the future benefits, warn of the consequences of inaction, or bolster your own credentials. Here are some guidelines to add depth to your evidence and have it be heard more clearly.

Data: Specifics Encourage Engagement

People equate specificity with certainty, so precise evidence is far more powerful than generalities. When evidence is specific, it allows comparison and judgment, engaging others in a mental process rather than treating them as passive receptors.

Al Clausi, president of the Institute of Food Technologists, was an advocate for food research. As such, he had to develop a Guide that would engage his constituents. To support his advocacy, Clausi added a few specific pieces of information:

> Food is our nation's largest manufacturing sector. The annual value of shipments by the nation's 16,000 food manufacturers approaches $400 billion. Adding value to raw farm commodities, by processing them into foods, employs 1.5 million Americans. In 1991 we contributed $145 billion in "added value" to our domestic economy. That compares with chemicals, including pharmaceutical, that contributed $155 billion, and transportation equipment, including cars, that contributed $152 billion.

Later, to support the need to promote health and safety in foods, he added:

> If improved nutrition reduced health care costs by 10 percent . . . a realistic goal . . . the savings to the country would be $14.6 billion.[1]

This data was all specific, and therefore engaging and effective. The comparison of the food industry to other industries (drugs and cars) that were known by his constituents also provided a meaningful yardstick for the statistics.

But what if Clausi had used only generalities, saying: "It is sufficient to say that the nation's food manufacturing sector is huge. It compares favorably with the chemical and transportation industry in its size and impact on American jobs and GDP." And later: "If improved nutrition reduced health care costs by a few percentage points, the results would be enormous."

It isn't hard to hear and feel the difference. Specificity enhances your credibility. It provides evidence that you are paying close attention to the issue, rather than merely reading a briefing book.

Relevance: Making Data Meaningful to Others

Frequently, the relationship of the data to others is not at all clear. In those cases, rather than letting people struggle with the relevance, you can tell them directly what it means.

At my younger son's university graduation, the chancellor took his obligatory turn at the microphone and used ten minutes to encourage our financial support of higher education. He used data to substantiate the excellence of the school, naming the number of Nobel laureates on the faculty and the amount of research money they were able to attract. He used statistics, comparing the amount of research money procured by the university to like numbers from other top universities in the United States.

It was interesting, but not engaging. As I surveyed the audience of students and parents with my speech critic's eye, I could see that the level of attention was due to the audience's pride in accomplishment, not because of any impressive thoughts or inspiring messages from the chancellor.

Finally, he remarked on the increased competition to gain admission to the university that had resulted from its enhanced reputation. He quoted the minimum combination of SAT score and grade point average required for admission four years previously, and compared it to the same standard today. It was much tougher to gain admission today than it had been in past years. He then commented: "This means if you look to your left and your right, one of the two people you see, your fellow graduates, would not be admitted to this institution if they were applying today."

The atmosphere in the audience immediately changed. The chancellor had made it possible for each person to directly experience the relevance of the data. As I was listening and watching the students look right and left, I was also wondering if my son would have been one of those who would still gain admission. My mind immediately made the data personal, and as a result, I felt a much closer connection to the statistics—and a much closer connection to the speech and the speaker.

Global Data Made Local

A third effective way of making contextual data relevant is to express it in terms of a familiar setting. If the evidence is global, or in a context that is not familiar to the audience, the numbers can be cast in a more commonplace background.

Timothy Wirth, assistant secretary of state under Bill Clinton, cited the following statistics in a speech on sustainable development delivered to the Washington Press Club: "And in China, home to one in five of the earth's people, severe water shortages and soil erosion threaten that nation's ability to sustain its population. Between 1957 and 1990, China lost nearly 70 million acres of cropland, *an area the size of all the farms in France, Germany, Denmark and the Netherlands combined.*"[2]

Wirth expressed the data in a frame (Northern Europe) that was more familiar to his audience than China. Given that his constituency was made up exclusively of Americans, he could have been even more effective had he related the loss in China to a land area in the United States; for example North Dakota, Nebraska, and Kansas.

Data is an essential part of the justification for change. However, it can be communicated in a way that includes others, encourages the interaction with them, and adds to their respect and trust for the leader.

Quotations from Authorities: Support for Ideas

As you develop your Guide, you will often quote an authority who agrees with your ideas as a way of adding weight to your evidence—and occasionally to deepen your connection with others. But done without reflection, quoting can also damage both aspects of your credibility. For example, it is a common mistake to quote a philosopher, academic, or other expert without really knowing his work; or worse, to quote a person unknown to the audience, leaving them wondering about their own intelligence. You can seem arrogant and aloof when this occurs.

Consider these references to authority in Timothy Wirth's speech. Referring to the danger of the increasing use of natural resources, Wirth said: "Professor Tad Homer-Dixon of the University of Toronto warns that in the coming decades, quote, 'resource scarcities will probably occur with a speed, complexity and magnitude unprecedented in history.' " Wirth went on, "Current conflicts offer a grim foreshadowing of Robert Kaplan's coming anarchy, the anarchy that could engulf more and more nations if we fail to act." These obscure references to Homer-Dixon and Kaplan damaged Wirth's credibility rather than supporting his case. He verbally stumbled over the references, and chances are very good that most of the audience had not heard of at least one of his authorities. How could he have made these references more authoritative and authentic?

First, by assuring his own familiarity with the authorities, and second, by explaining their credentials to the audience. For example:

> Professor Tad Homer-Dixon of the University of Toronto is one of the world's authorities on environmental security. He has authored several widely read articles on how environmental problems can lead to conflict in developing countries, and was a keynote speaker at the U.N. conference on population and development in Cairo. Professor Dixon says, and I quote, "resource scarcities will probably occur with a speed, complexity and magnitude unprecedented in history."

Wirth could have augmented his reference to Kaplan as well:

> Current conflicts offer a grim foreshadowing of a coming anarchy that could engulf more and more nations if we fail to act, an anarchy foretold by Robert Kaplan in his recent frightening cover article in the *Atlantic Monthly*.

By expanding and clarifying these references, Wirth would have strengthened *his own* credentials and would have shown more respect for his audience.

Experts Who Are Real

It is possible to deepen the connection with others even further by relating your relationship with the expert. Did you read the works of Bertrand Russell as a teenager growing up in the Bronx? Did your father talk to you about life on fall evenings on the porch in San Diego? Did you read every speech that John F. Kennedy ever delivered? Did you study Zen koans at a temple in Kyoto? Explaining the source of your respect for the authority deepens the level of intimacy with others, adding to your credibility and your humanity, encouraging their engagement with you and the change you are advocating.

Many of the greatest lessons I have learned have come from people who are close to me and who have gained their expertise through *experience.* When I quote these people, I am also sharing a part of my life with the audience, and they sense the authenticity in that sharing. For example, I know a woman minister who began attending seminary in her late thirties. She had been successful in business for the previous fifteen years, but had been unhappy with what she perceived as a constant moral dilemma. The decision to give up her career was not easy. She asked everyone she trusted for advice, prayed about her decision every day, even sought professional counseling on the issue, but could not gather the courage to make a decision. Finally, at an evening meeting at the church, she announced that despite a severe shortage of resources and not having a place to live, she was going to leave her job and enroll in seminary for the fall term.

A month later, this woman was back at the church for the same group meeting. By then she had secured a scholarship and a place in the student housing center. All the resources she needed had become available as soon as she had made her decision. That second night she told us, "I always thought that I needed clarity to create commitment, but now I realize that it is the other way around—it is commitment that creates clarity!"

I use this story as evidence whenever I discuss the power of commitment. It never fails to connect me with others and to add a great deal of authority to my remarks. The quotation is not merely an abstraction that I read in some book. The power of the quotation is both in the words, which may be seen as universally true, and in the obvious impact on me, the advocate. Other people appreciate the intimacy inherent in quoting someone I know personally. I was there, the woman was real to me, and that reality gets transmitted to the audience.

Authentic leaders collect the writings and sayings of those people who have actually had an impact on their own lives, not the most popular people, or even the most noted authorities (although these categories can overlap). When they quote those authorities, they also include the circumstances of discovering the citation. Such authenticity adds immeasurably to the power of the supplemental authority.

Applying these rules of evidence will enhance the clarity of your message to others, making it more relevant and meaningful and adding to their recognition of your competence and empathy.

Appendix B

Framework for Personal Leadership Communication Guide

1. Establishing competence and building trustworthiness
    - Competence
        - Clarity of purpose
            Problem
            Specific change advocated
            Evidence of compelling need
            Broad implications; value represented
        - Credentials and vulnerabilities
    - Trustworthiness
        - Displaying empathy
            Expressing gratitude
            Acknowledging resistance
            Finding commonality in purpose
        - Willingness to be known
            Personal motivation, personal value
2. Creating shared context
    - History
    - Priority
    - Current reality (include barriers)
    - Reinforcing competence and trust
    - Articulating a broader perspective

3. Declaring and describing the future: an act of creation . . .
    - Vivid picture, sensory-rich images
    - Stakes (If we do . . . If we don't. . . .)
    - Values expressed either way
4. Committing to action
    - Steps (organizational)
    - Personal commitment, personal action
    - Request for action (specific)

Notes

Part One

1. BlessingWhite: *External* attunement is the penchant of the leader to listen to others' points of view. This differs from *empathy,* which is the ability to put yourself in someone else's shoes, or feel what they are feeling. *Depth* deals with the creation of meaning from the task ahead, rather than merely stating the desired result. See *Empathy Matters Most for Effective Leadership,* December 26, 2007; available online: www.blessingwhite.com/docDescription.asp?id=216&pid=6&sid=1
2. Daniel H. Pink, *Drive: The Surprising Truth About What Motivates Us* (London: Penguin, 2009). For further information, see works by Edward Deci and Richard Flaste, *Why We Do What We Do* (New York: Penguin, 1996) and Dan Ariely, *The Honest Truth About Dishonesty* (New York: HarperCollins, 2012).
3. William Deresiewicz, "Solitude and Leadership," *American Scholar,* Spring 2010.

Chapter 1

1. W. Bennis et al., "Learning Some Basic Truisms About Leadership," in *The New Paradigm in Business,* edited by M. Ray and A. Rinzler (New York: Putnam, 1993), p. 77.
2. W. Bennis, *On Becoming a Leader* (Boston: Addison-Wesley, 1992), p. 122.
3. " 'You've got to find what you love,' Jobs says," Stanford Report, June 14, 2005; available online: http://news.stanford.edu/news/2005/june15/jobs-061505
4. M. Cuomo, *More Than Words: The Speeches of Mario Cuomo* (New York: St. Martin's Press, 1993), pp. xvi, xviii.
5. J. Hillman and M. Ventura, *We've Had a Hundred Years of Psychotherapy—and the World's Getting Worse* (San Francisco: Harper, 1992), p. 53.
6. H. Schultz and D. Jones Yang, *Pour Your Heart into It* (New York: Hyperion, 1997), pp. 3, 4.

Chapter 2

1. P. Ekman, *Emotions Revealed* (New York: St. Martin's Press, 2003).
2. T. Lewis, F. Amini, and R. Lannon, *A General Theory of Love* (New York: Random House, 2000).
3. Sydney Lumet, director, *Twelve Angry Men;* screenplay by Reginald Rose; produced by Reginald Rose and Henry Fonda; distributed by United Artists, 1957.
4. V. Emery, *The Pentium Chip Story: A Learning Experience,* n.d.; available online: www.emery.com/1e/pentium.htm
5. Emery, *The Pentium Chip Story.*
6. V. Emery, *Dr. Andrew Grove's Pentium Email,* November 27, 1994; available online: www.emery.com/library/grove.htm
7. R. J. Davidson, with Sharon Begley, *The Emotional Life of Your Brain* (New York: Penguin, 2012).
8. D. S. Pottruck and T. Pearce, *Clicks and Mortar: Passion Driven Growth in an Internet Driven World* (San Francisco: Jossey-Bass, 2000), pp. 92–93.
9. D. Goleman, *Emotional Intelligence* (New York: Bantam Books, 1995), p. 28.
10. Jim Collins, *Good to Great: Why Some Companies Make the Leap . . . and Others Don't* (New York: HarperBusiness, 2001), p. 74.

Chapter 3

1. For more general discussion of brain function as it relates to human connection, see Robert K. Cooper and Ayman Sawaf, *Executive EQ* (New York: Grosset Putnam, 1996) and T. Lewis, F. Amini, and R. Lannon, *A General Theory of Love* (New York: Random House, 2000).
2. Lewis, Amini, and Lannon, *A General Theory of Love,* p. 64.
3. A. M. Paul, "Your Brain on Fiction," *New York Times,* March 17, 2012; available online: www.nytimes.com/2012/03/18/opinion/sunday/the-neuroscience-of-your-brain-on-fiction.html
4. Paul, "Your Brain on Fiction."
5. C. G. Jung, *Approaching the Unconscious: Man and His Symbols,* edited by Carl Jung (New York: Dell, 1964), p. 3.
6. Jung, *Approaching the Unconscious.*
7. J. Joyce, *A Portrait of the Artist as a Young Man* (New York: Viking, 1964). Originally published 1916.
8. M. Felberbaum, "Judge Blocks Graphic Images on Cigarette Packages," Associated Press, February 29, 2012; available online: http://news.yahoo.com/judge-blocks-graphic-images-cigarette-packages-195944976.html

9. For a thorough discussion of the metaphor as a descriptor of business, see Gareth Morgan, *Images of Organization* (Thousand Oaks, CA: Sage, 1997).
10. R. Mahoney, "Politics, Technology, and Economic Growth," *Vital Speeches of the Day* 59, no. 20 (1993): 627.
11. D. Goldin, "The Light of a New Age," *Vital Speeches of the Day* 58 no. 24 (1992): 741.
12. H. Arendt, *Men in Dark Times* (New York: Harcourt Brace, 1983), p. 147.
13. J. Campbell, *Pathways to Bliss: Mythology and Personal Transformation*, edited by David Kudler (Novato, CA: New World Library, 2004), p. 7.
14. Campbell, *Pathways to Bliss*, p. 8.
15. Campbell, *Pathways to Bliss*, p. 9.
16. J. Martin and M. E. Power, "Organizational Stories: More Vivid and Persuasive Than Quantitative Data," in *Psychological Foundations of Organizational Behavior*, edited by B. M. Staw (Glenview, IL: Scott, Foresman, 1982), 161–168; also see J. M. Kouzes and B. P. Posner, *Credibility: How Leaders Gain and Lose It, Why People Demand It* (San Francisco: Jossey-Bass, 1993).

Chapter 4

1. J. Lehrer, *How We Decide* (New York: Houghton Mifflin Harcourt, 2009), pp. 248–249.
2. D. Walcott, *Collected Poems 1948–1984* (New York: Farrar, Straus & Giroux, 1986), p. 328.
3. Stanley Kunitz, "The Layers," in *Wild Braid* (New York: Norton, 2007).
4. For Louv's work, see *The Last Child in the Woods* (New York: Algonquin Books, 2005) and *The Nature Principle* (New York: Algonquin Books, 2011).
5. R. Commanday, "Repin Flawless in Technique," *San Francisco Chronicle*, Dec. 12, 1992, "Datebook," p. 32.

Part Two

1. M. Cuomo, *More Than Words: The Speeches of Mario Cuomo* (New York: St. Martin's Press, 1993), p. xvii.

Chapter 5

1. F. D. Raines, "Racial Inequality in America," *Vital Speeches of the Day* 68, no. 13 (2002): 400.

2. R. S. Butler, "Planning for Death in a Century of Cure," Haas School of Business, speech presented in Berkeley, CA, March 22, 2002.
3. E. M. Kennedy, "Eliminating the Threat: The Right Course of Action for Disarming Iraq, Combating Terrorism, Protecting the Homeland, and Stabilizing the Middle East," September 27, 2002; available online: http://media.sais-jhu.edu/archive/podcast/senator-edward-kennedy-d-mass-eliminating-threat-right-course-action-disarming-iraq-combatin
4. M. Cuomo, *More Than Words: The Speeches of Mario Cuomo* (New York: St. Martin's Press, 1993), p. 35.
5. R. K. Cooper and A. Sawaf, *Executive EQ* (New York: Grosset Putnam, 1996), p. 100.
6. J. F. Kennedy, "Commencement Address at American University in Washington," June 10, 1963; available online: www.ratical.org/co-globalize/JFK061063.html
7. B. Jordan, videotaped speech (New York: National Broadcasting Company, 1997).

Chapter 6

1. G. Lakoff, *Don't Think of an Elephant* (White River Junction, VT: Chelsea Green, 2004).
2. H. Nouwen, *The Genesee Diary* (New York: Image Books, 1976), p. 113.
3. S. J. Gould, "The Strike That Was High and Outside," *New York Times,* section 1, November 19, 1984. p. 23.
4. P. Senge, *The Fifth Discipline: The Art and Practice of the Learning Organization* (New York: Doubleday, 1990), p. 354.
5. D. Seidman, *How: Why How We Do Anything Means Everything . . . in Business (and in Life)* (Hoboken, NJ: Wiley, 2007), p. xxiv.
6. J. Adams, "Juggling Job and Family," *Vital Speeches of the Day* 60, no. 4 (1994): 125.
7. B. Moyers, *Healing and the Mind* (audiocassette) (Bantam Books Audio, February 1993).
8. R. S. Butler, "Planning for Death in a Century of Cure," speech presented at the Haas School of Business, Berkeley, CA, March 22, 2002.

Chapter 7

1. Schaar quote available online: www.goodreads.com/quotes/show/279924
2. B. Gwertzman, "The Official View on Iceland Is Still Chilly, but Thawing," *New York Times,* section 4 (October 19, 1986): 1.
3. "Obama Prague Speech on Nuclear Weapons: Full Text," Huff Post Politics, May 25, 2011; available online: www.huffingtonpost.com/2009/04/05/obama-prague-speech-on-nu_n_183219.html

4. O. Wilde, *The Wit and Humor of Oscar Wilde,* edited by Alvan Redman (New York: Dover, 1959), p. 191.
5. A. de Saint-Exupéry, *The Wisdom of Sands (French title Citadelle),* translated by S. Gilbert (Orlando, FL: Harcourt Brace, 1950), section 89.
6. James C. Collins and Jerry I. Porras, *Built to Last* (San Francisco: Harper Business, 1994).
7. Quoted in Bai, Matt. "Still Waiting for the Narrator in Chief", *New York Times Magazine,* Nov 12, 2012. Pp. 17.
8. Ibid.

Chapter 8

1. Ch'êng-ên Wu, *Monkey,* translated by Arthur Waley (New York: Grove Press, 1984).
2. R. W. Terry, *Authentic Leadership: Courage in Action* (San Francisco: Jossey-Bass, 1993), p. 13.
3. M. Avallone, *A Woman Called Golda* (New York: Leisure Books, 1982), pp. 164–165.

Chapter 9

1. Edward Hallowell, "The Human Moment at Work," *Harvard Business Review,* 77 (Jan/Feb 1999): 58–66.
2. Thomas Lewis, conversation with the author at the Forum on Cross-Cultural Inspiration in San Francisco, January 2007.

Appendix A

1. A. Clausi, "U.S. Food System Needs for the Twenty-First Century," *Vital Speeches of the Day* 60, no. 17 (1994): 542.
2. T. Wirth, "Global Conditions," *National Press Club speech presented in Washington, D.C.,* July 12, (1994).

Recommended Reading

Those interested in the subjects discussed in *Leading Out Loud* may find further value in the following readings. The list on leadership development is rudimentary, the others are a bit broader. The list reflects only my personal preferences.

Leadership Development

Deresiewicz, W. "Solitude and Leadership." *American Scholar,* March 1, 2010.

Gardner, J. W. *On Leadership.* New York: Free Press, 1993.

Gardner, J. W. *Self-Renewal: The Individual and Innovative Society. Reissued ed.* New York: Norton, 1995.

Goffee, R., and Jones, G. *Why Should Anyone Be Led by You? What It Takes to Be an Authentic Leader.* Boston: Harvard Business Review Press, 2006.

Heifitz, R. *Leadership Without Easy Answers.* Cambridge, MA: Belknap Press of Harvard University Press, 1994.

Kouzes, J., and Posner, B. *The Leadership Challenge,* 4th ed. San Francisco: Jossey-Bass, 1995.

Leonard, G. *Mastery: The Keys to Success and Long-Term Fulfillment.* New York: Dutton, 1991.

Miller, W. C. *Flash of Brilliance.* New York: Perseus Books, 1999.

Pottruck, D., and Pearce, T. *Clicks and Mortar: Passion Driven Growth in an Internet Driven World.* San Francisco: Jossey-Bass, 2000.

Quinn, R. *Deep Change: Discovering the Leader Within.* San Francisco: Jossey-Bass, 1996.

Seidman, D. *How: Why How We Do Anything Means Everything.* Hoboken, NJ: Wiley, 2007.

Steindl-Rast, Br. D. *Gratefulness, the Heart of Prayer.* Mahwah, NJ: Paulist Press, 1984.

Terry, R. W. *Authentic Leadership: Courage in Action.* San Francisco: Jossey-Bass, 1993.

Neuroscience and Leadership

Ariely, D. *The Honest Truth About Dishonesty.* New York: HarperCollins, 2012.

Cohen, P. "Next Big Thing in English: Knowing They Know That You Know." *New York Times,* April 1, 2010.

Deci, E., and Flaste, R. *Why We Do What We Do.* New York: Penguin, 1996.

Iacoboni, M. *Mirroring People: The New Science of How We Connect With Others.* New York: Farrar, Straus, & Giroux, 2008.

Lehrer, J. *How We Decide.* New York: HarperCollins, 2012.

Lewis, T., Amini, F., and Lannon, R. *A General Theory of Love.* New York: Random House, 2000.

Pink, D. H. *Drive: The Surprising Truth About What Motivates Us.* New York: Riverhead Books, 2009.

Ringleb, A. H., and Rock, D. "NeuroLeadership in 2009." *NeuroLeadership Journal* (Sydney, Australia) 2 (2009): 2–8.

Siegel, D. J. *The Mindful Brain: Reflection and Attunement in the Cultivation of Well-Being.* New York: Norton, 2007.

Siegel, D. J. *Mindsight: The New Science of Personal Transformation.* New York: Random House, 2010.

Emotional Intelligence

Cooper, R., and Sawaf, A. *Executive EQ.* New York: Grosset-Putnam, 1997.

Goleman, D. *Emotional Intelligence.* New York: Bantam Books, 1995.

Goleman, D., et al. *Primal Leadership: Realizing the Power of Emotional Intelligence.* Boston: Harvard Business School Press, 2002.

Goleman, D. (Nar.). *Destructive Emotions: A Scientific Dialogue with the Dalai Lama.* New York: Bantam, 2003.

Oatley, K., Keltner, D., and Jenkins, J. M. *Understanding Emotions,* 2nd ed. Hoboken, NJ: Wiley-Blackwell, 2006.

Organizational Effectiveness

Marlow, F., Masarech, M., and Rice, C. *The Engagement Equation: Leadership Strategies for an Inspired Workforce.* Hoboken, NJ: Wiley, 2012.

Morgan, G. *Images of Organizations.* Thousand Oaks, CA: Sage, 1997.

Neuhauser, P. *Tribal Warfare in Organizations.* New York: HarperBusiness, 1988.

Senge, P. *The Fifth Discipline: The Art and Practice of the Learning Organization.* New York: Doubleday, 1990.

Whyte, D. *The Heart Aroused: Poetry and Preservation of the Soul in Corporate America.* New York: Currency Doubleday, 1994.

Context, Myth, Culture

Campbell, J. *The Hero with a Thousand Faces,* 2nd ed. Princeton, NJ: Princeton University Press, 1973.

Collins, B. *Sailing Alone Around the Room.* New York: Random House, 2001.

Fisher, W. R. *Human Communication as Narration: Toward a Philosophy of Reason, Value, and Action.* Columbia: University of South Carolina Press, 1989.

Frazer, J. G. *The Golden Bough.* New York: Macmillan, 1922.

Freidman, T. *The Lexus and the Olive Tree.* New York: Farrar, Straus, & Giroux, 1999, and other Freidman publications.

Gergen, K. *The Saturated Self: Dilemmas of Identity in Contemporary Life.* New York: Basic Books, 1991.

Handy, C. *The Age of Unreason.* Boston: Harvard Business School Press, 1990.

Handy, C. *The Hungry Spirit.* New York: Broadway Books, 1998.

Kopping, K.-P. *Adolf Bastian and the Psychic Unity of Mankind: The Foundations of Anthropology in Nineteenth Century Germany.* Berlin: LIT Verlag, 2005.

Nouwen, H. *The Genesee Diary: Report from a Trappist Monastery.* New York: Image Books, 1976.

Shenk, D. *Data Smog: Surviving the Information Glut.* San Francisco: Harper Edge, 1997.

Tarnas, R. *The Passion of the Western Mind: Understanding the Ideas That Have Shaped Our World View.* New York: Harmony Books: 1991.

Taylor, J., and Wacker, W. *The 500-Year Delta.* New York: Harper Business, 1997.

Wishard, W. Van D. *Between Two Ages: The 21st Century and the Crisis of Meaning.* Reston, VA: WorldTrends Research, 2000.

Zimmer, H. *Myths and Symbols in Indian Art and Civilization* (Joseph Campbell, ed.). Princeton, NJ: Princeton University Press, 1946.

Philosophical Foundations

Frankl, V. E. *Man's Search for Meaning.* New York: Pocket Books, 1963.

Keen, S. *The Passionate Life: Stages of Loving.* San Francisco: Harper & Row, 1983.

Milosz, C. (ed.). *A Book of Luminous Things.* Orlando, FL: Harcourt Brace & Company, 1996.

Mitchell, S. (ed.). *The Enlightened Heart.* New York: Harper & Row, 1989.

Mitchell, S. (ed.). *The Enlightened Mind.* New York: HarperCollins, 1991.

Needleman, J. *Money and the Meaning of Life.* New York: Doubleday, 1991.

Needleman, J. *A Little Book on Love.* New York: Currency Doubleday, 1996.

Needleman, J. *Time and the Soul: Where Has All the Meaningful Time Gone—and Can We Get It Back?* San Francisco: Berrett-Koehler, 2003.

Osborn, D. (ed.). *Reflections on the Art of Living, A Joseph Campbell Companion.* New York: HarperCollins, 1991.

Rilke, R. M. *Letters to a Young Poet.* New York: Vintage Books, 1987. (Mitchell translation.)

Wilber, K. *Up from Eden.* Boston: Shambhala, 1983.

Wilber, K. *A Brief History of Everything.* Boston: Shambhala, 1996.

Wilber, K. *Integral Psychology: Consciousness, Spirit, Psychology, Therapy.* Boston: Shambhala, 2000.

Acknowledgments

First, a deep bow to Randy Komisar who graciously agreed to write a stirring foreword. He is a rare combination of teacher, entrepreneur, and spiritual adventurer who can give voice to all of those aspects at once. I'm lucky to call him friend.

Equally impressive is Jan Hunter, development editor and a true partner in bringing this work to print. Beyond sheer talent, she brings discernment, perspective, and caring to the task. This is a rare combination actually referred to in the text. She was the leader here. The book simply would not be, but for her.

Rita Becker had a similar impact in a different role, holding down the business with good cheer and aplomb while I struggled with the decisions and execution necessary to bring new material to life. I know I was a real pain for several months, a condition that she ignored in favor of her belief in what we do . . . just amazing.

Others contributed directly to the growth of the material by teaching it. My partners at BlessingWhite were central to this part of the evolution. In particular, Chris Rice, Chris Brunone, Matt Varava, Fraser Marlow, and Tom Barry, and in the trenches, Joan Dasher, Larry Seal, Stace Williams, Dave Hagerty, Karen Shylo, Bill Costello, Ann Mamallo, and Liz McLean-Brown. All have added immensely to our experience of engaging others in this process. Their contributions are reflected in the work.

Soon after the original version of this title was published, Christy Tonge expanded the ideas and reshaped *Leading Out Loud* from its book-type cocoon into a butterfly. For seventeen years she and her husband Barry have continued to inspire me with their lives. She is the perfect example of someone who uses the principles of this work.

So is Tina de Souza of São Paulo, Brazil. What a paragon of leadership, guiding a worldwide organization that does good for humankind, counseling others, running a school, supporting her family, and finding time to be my friend and confidante. She is the epitome of what this book tries to bring forth. I owe her a great debt for her support.

Spiritual counselors occasionally don't relate to the world as it is, but only how it could be. This is not the case for Richard Lannon, Baba Hariji, and Kim Soskin. Each in their own way have counseled me into actually writing this rather than just talking about it. Equally important, although not as frequent, were the words of Dennis Slattery and Brother David Steindl-Rast. It's hard to overstate their respective contributions.

I particularly want to thank those who shared their stories: John Bunch, Rebekah Saul Butler, Karen Chang, Rebecca DeCola, Pip Coburn, Michael Nahum, Ross Dove, Josie Gaillard, Tom Haverty, Matt Hyde, Ed Jensen, Mike McMullen, Tom Murphy, Rob Nicholson, Nick Roelofs, and John Ure. Their contributions brought the ideas to life, as did the effort of Nate Hayes who found many of them with meticulous research.

To my friend and partner, Dave Pottruck, and his wife Emily Scott-Pottruck, I offer my intense gratitude, my greatest thanks. Dave's personal use of the principles of *Leading Out Loud* and his confidence in teaching them in his own course at The Wharton School at the University of Pennsylvania has amplified their value. It has taken personal courage for him to do that, and I appreciate it.

And finally, the folks at Jossey-Bass just make it easy. My thanks particularly to Alison Hankey, Mark Karmendy, and Michael Kay, who applied just the right amount of understanding and professionalism to make the book real, and to Dani Scoville and Alina Poniewaz-Bolten who tracked and marshaled the myriad ancillary permissions and legal needs. Kudos, too, for Hilary Powers, the ever-sharp and ever-enthusiastic copy editor—a person with much to say and the wit to say it effectively and graciously. This new edition was actually more difficult to write than the original version or the second edition. It required a different filter to see and to distinguish what is new from what is really just a restatement of what I had said before in different words. It takes special people to put up with and contribute to the kind of craziness it requires to see this process through, and I am blessed with many such patient people in my life. To associates and friends—Leni Miller, Kathy Thulin, Diana Johnson, Tom Verkozen, Ed Bernbaum, and the whole left end at the MBC—thanks for not leaving.

To Sandra Hopkins, for love and support despite the stress, for long phone calls and many hugs. Back at you.

And finally to my family of J's. . . . Jeff, Joel, Jason, Jen, and the rebel, Alissa; and to all of their kiddles, my deepest love. The boys and I are going fishing again.

About the Author

Terry Pearce is founder and president of Leadership Communication, a company that coaches high-profile corporate, political, and social leaders on the principles of the art of creating inspiration. He is widely credited for distinguishing leadership communication as a separate field in the mid-1990s.

The content and method of his coaching and consulting are radical departures from conventional wisdom, and are designed to move people to commitment rather than mere compliance, resulting in higher levels of contribution and innovation. His clients include executives, public officials, and high-level teams of Fortune 500 companies and more recently leaders of new companies that are changing the world.

Until 2005, Terry was an adjunct professor at the Haas Business School at the University of California, Berkeley, where his courses received the highest ratings from graduate students for providing useful, effective, and relevant tools for their futures as leaders in the business community, and for assisting them to explore themes that were meaningful as a life's work. He has been a visiting lecturer at the London School of Business in the Sloan fellowship program and a contributor to the Executive Briefing Video Series at Stanford University.

Terry is particularly interested in inspiration as it applies to the entire human family, regardless of culture. He earned a master's in comparative mythology and became a doctoral candidate at the Pacifica Graduate Institute at the age of sixty-four. He continues to speak and consult to groups about leadership communication and its role in shifting perception and instilling inspiration for change. His corporate partner, BlessingWhite, is a leading consultancy in employee engagement and leadership.

Together, Terry and BlessingWhite use his material with international clients.

Terry's avid interest and commitment to the relationship between leadership and communication began as a student leader at Linfield College in Oregon, where he earned a bachelor of science degree in business with a strong emphasis in religious philosophy.

For the first seventeen years of his career, Terry was a manager and executive at IBM. During the 1980s he pioneered U.S. business activities in the Soviet Union as co-founder of Partners, a firm that marketed consumer products and facilitated joint industrial projects in Russia. This experience sharpened his interest in the possibility of inspiration as a universal phenomenon.

From 1994 until 2002, he also served as a fellow and a senior vice president of executive communication for Charles Schwab Corporation.

Terry's writings include the business bestseller *Clicks and Mortar: Passion Driven Growth in an Internet-Driven World* (coauthored with David Pottruck) and *Leading Out Loud,* hailed by "Executive Summaries" as one of the thirty best business books of 1995, and as "one of the best books on speaking ever written." It was revised and broadened in 2003 to include all forms of communication. This current version incorporates learning and experiences from his subsequent graduate education and worldwide experience as a speaker, leadership communication consultant, and teacher.

Active in the community, Terry was the founding director of the Partnership for a Drug-Free California, and in 1989 ran across the United States as a member of "Transcon 89" to promote this cause. He is former chairman of the board of the National Endowment for Financial Education, and a board member of Up With People, and of A Network for Grateful Living. He currently serves on the boards of the Pacifica Graduate Institute and Center Point, a substance-abuse nonprofit. He has two living children and six grandchildren and lives in Northern California.

Index

Terry Pearce

Leadership Communication™

Leading Out Loud is the basis for graduate courses taught at numerous universities around the world. Through his company and with his corporate partner BlessingWhite, Terry Pearce teaches the principles of *Leading Out Loud* in a number of different formats, and consults with executives and other leaders in preparing Leadership Communication Guides.

If you are interested in more information about Leadership Communication, about using *Leading Out Loud* as the basis for a university course, or if you have stories of inspirational communication you would like to share, please call us at 415-464-0520 or visit our virtual home at www.terrypearce.com.

TERRY PEARCE
LEADERSHIP COMMUNICATION™

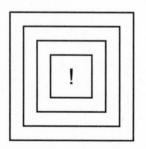

You've Read the Book, What's Next?

For more than thirty-five years, BlessingWhite has helped organizations develop more effective leaders. Through our partnership with Terry Pearce, we are privileged to offer a leadership development experience like no other, designed to help managers and leaders use themselves as powerful vehicles for effecting positive strategic and operational change in organizations. Leading Out Loud™ provides the discipline and a practical communication framework to more deeply connect with and inspire others in this competitive, uncertain business environment.

Leading Out Loud™ helps organizations to:

- Create authentic leaders who inspire willing, committed action by others.
- Raise the standard for the candid, constructive conversations that spur innovation and courage.